TONY WAITERS
COACHING
YOUTH
SOCCER

A & C Black · London

Published 1990 by
A & C Black (Publishers) Ltd
35 Bedford Row, London WC1R 4JH

First published 1984 under the title
Coaching to Win: Soccer for the young player
by Totem Books, a division of Collins Publishers,
Ontario, Canada

© 1984, 1990 Tony Waiters

ISBN 0 7136 3319 0

A CIP catalogue record of this book is available
from the British Library.

The soccer ball logo used to designate
youngsters' parents' and coaches' sections of
each chapter is © World of Soccer.

Printed and bound in Great Britain by
BPCC Hazell Books, Aylesbury, Bucks.

To my Mum and Dad for all their encouragement and belief; to brother Mick – my first coach and best friend; to Verdi Godwin who got me into Pro. Soccer and has continued to inspire me ever since; to Anne – my secretary, adviser, taskmaster and wife; to my son Scott that he can enjoy the great game of soccer as I have; to my daughter Victoria that she can please herself!

Contents

Acknowledgments

Nike International, Baden, Simon Fraser University, Belaire Celtic Soccer Team, Blue Mountain Soccer Club, Glen Davies, Ron Paton, Richard Dinnis, Bob Bearpark, Alan Hinton, Alan Churchard, Les Wilson.

FOREWORD

The Tony Waiters' story

Being brought up in Britain in the aftermath of World War II and living 20 miles from Liverpool made it almost inevitable that soccer would be part of my life even before I could kick a ball straight. In those days there was no television, motorcars belonged exclusively to the rich, and to see professional soccer was a treat reserved for the infrequent occasions when Dad took brother Mick and me to a game. That would be to watch Southport Football Club of the English Third Division North, or very occasionally to Anfield, home of the mighty Liverpool Club (although not so mighty in those days as they laboured in the Second Division!).

There were other times, too, when my boyhood gang of friends amassed enough pennies – selling firewood was our main money-raiser – to pay for the train ride, bus fare and admission fee to the Southport stadium. (To be truthful, on occasions we bypassed the turnstiles in favour of a less orthodox and less expensive entry through the crumbling fences of the Haig Avenue ground!)

We also saw the best of soccer when we went to the "flicks". The big international games were an absolute must for the newsreels of the day. And at that time, England was still recognised not only as the father of soccer, but also as the strongest soccer-playing nation in the world.

Apart from increasing my knowledge of the game through those rare glimpses at professionals playing it, I also learned much from what people actually told me about soccer, and from the newspapers. The back pages of nearly all traditional British papers were – and still are today – the preserve of sport. So after Dad finished with the paper I'd grab it, find a quiet spot, and then read it from the back. Not that I'd make it to the front page news. Who cared about the Cold War situation, when Manchester United had unjuries to four key players? I was always captivated by the photographs. Looking at them, I would study the way a player headed a ball, struck a pass or shot for goal, and how a goalkeeper dived to make a save.

As brother Mick and I grew up together, we took every opportunity to get outside with some sort of soccer ball – even a tennis ball. (There was a distinct shortage of affordable soccer balls after the war.) We played in the streets, in the back yard, in the open fields, anywhere. And whenever Mick and I played soccer together, I was the goalkeeper. We spent many happy hours, just the two of us, playing soccer, with Mick shooting for goal and me trying to stop the shot. We'd pretend that Mick was Liverpool, Arsenal or Manchester United, and I was Newcastle, or Manchester City, or Everton. Every great save counted as a goal for me, every authentic goal from Mick's boots scored for him. Most of the games were fiercely fought, closely scored, and aggressively argued. They were great times, great fun, and great practice – certainly for me.

Our gang had the good fortune to live in a village, although Ainsdale was on the fringe of the town of Southport. You would hardly know that today, as Southport has merged with and completely absorbed Ainsdale. One mile to the west of the village was the beach – mile upon mile of it, washed twice a day by the tides as they rolled in for two miles and then flowed out again, leaving behind natural sand soccer pitches. (Practice time on the beach had to be set by the tide-tables!) Half a mile to the north of our homes was Blundells Fields: four square miles of wild, gently undulating grassland with just one tamed area – a soccer field.

The Luftwaffe had greatly assisted our recreational facilities when in 1944, a German bomber chased off-course by an RAF Spitfire dropped its cargo 200 yards from our home. The back wall of our house factured and needed rebuilding, but the rest remained largely intact. Six other houses closer to where the bomb landed weren't so lucky, including the mansion house of the village with its own three acres of garden and a tennis court. The inhabitants were forced to evacuate. Our gang moved in and the tennis court became the perfect four-a-side soccer field.

There were a million things we boys could do around Ainsdale, what with the bombed houses, Blundells Fields, fine forests, miles of sandhills, and the beach. We only realise now that for youngsters, it was Utopia. All the same, soccer was the dominant recreation.

Mainly we played three versus three or four versus four. We made believe we were playing in the great stadia of England – at Anfield, Wembley, Old Trafford, Highbury. And we were playing for great teams – Liverpool, Tottenham, Manchester United, and England!

I wanted to be a soccer player so badly that the "eleven-plus" examination – a feature then of the English educational system – became a great worry in my young life. It wasn't the academic side that distressed me so much as the fear of my parting company with soccer. The all-important eleven-plus was an examination that every child was compelled to sit in the state schools of England. The results determined the direction a youngster's secondary education would take: pass and you went into the elitist grammar school system; fail and you were committed to a secondary modern school which, almost by definition, provided a second class education. I bragged to my friends that I was going to deliberately fail the eleven-plus because the grammar schools played rugby while the secondary modern schools offered soccer as the main sport.

However, I passed the eleven-plus and grew to love rugby in spite of my initial misgivings. But the game would always come second for me – a long way behind soccer. There were no real conflicts with regard to playing both games until I was 14 and selected to play in the Southport Schools Representative Soccer Team. The grammar school magnanimously allowed its rugby-playing students to represent the town soccer team as long as matches did not conflict with school rugby games. Thus I spent many Saturdays racing from a morning soccer game to a rugby game – a situation which became particularly complicated when one or both of the games were played out of town.

A worse dilemma faced me at 16, when I started playing in youth soccer with Southport Leyland Road. The Southport and District Youth League played its game at the same time as the school rugby team – Saturday afternoons. An old pal had once told me that if you tapped your knee with a silver spoon, it would cause swelling without inhibiting the functioning of the joint. I tried it. It didn't look particularly convincing, either to me or to Bob Abram, the rugby teacher. Nevertheless, I withdrew "injured" from the rugby team one particular Friday. Unfortunately, Mr Abram spotted me the next day as I sprinted for the bus to the soccer park and the youth game. On the Monday morning back at school, I was hauled in front of the Sports Committee, suspended from all school sports for four months, and compelled to attend all of our rugby matches to act as the line judge! No rugby, no freedom, and worse – no soccer!

After grammar school, I enrolled at the Loughborough College of Physical Education. To become a physical education teacher was, in my opinion, the next best thing to becoming a professional soccer player. But in between school and college, two years' compulsory National Service found me in the Royal Air Force. I wasn't flown off to an air base in some romantic corner of the world. Instead, I spent most of my time in the northeast of England at a smaller radar station, RAF Seaton Snook, near Middlesborough.

The northeast of England – Northumberland and Durham – is a region which has consistently produced great soccer players. Its heavily industrialised environment and the depression years of the 1930s which had hit this corner of England harder than any other, not only failed to inhibit the flow of soccer talent, some argue that these things cultivated the players.

For the first time in my life, despite the requirements of Her Majesty's Air Force, soccer became almost a complete way of life. Working my way right up to Middlesborough Reserves of the North Eastern League,

I truly became a part of soccer in the region. I suspect the knowledge that I would be going to Loughborough College after my National Service was not the reason why Middlesborough F.C. of the English Second Division chose not to offer me a professional contract. I was on their amateur books for a full season, attended the Tuesday and Thursday evening training sessions regularly, and participated as a reserve team player. I suspect they did not think I was good enough, though they never told me. At the time, they were probably right!

Loughborough was a great experience for me and a significant learning period in my life. Looking at "skills learning" in an objective, although at times academic, way was a valuable discipline. The importance of preparation for any coaching or teaching situation really hit home. Fortunately, prior to entering my third year at Loughborough, I had tryouts with Blackpool F.C. and Nottingham Forest, both of the English First Division. The two clubs asked me to sign with them and I chose Blackpool – as an amateur.

Unfortunately, the college would not allow me to travel to play with Blackpool, 120 miles away. There *were* Saturday morning lectures. So I quit Loughborough and signed as a professional with Blackpool F.C. – one of the best decisions of my life. Imagine actually being paid to do something you love!

The rest of my professional soccer career is in the record books. Not that I was ever the world's greatest soccer player or coach. It's the experiences that *can't* be found in the records, however, that have resulted in this book. Experiences such as taking my first coaching certification course during my first professional season at Blackpool, under the care and concern of ex-rugby player and Football Association Staff Coach, Arthur Etchells. The coaching in the Lancashire schools, whether as an official instructor of the Lancashire Football Association or as an unpaid volunteer. My one year's part-time teaching position at the Haweside School in Blackpool, where in addition to classroom work, I volunteered to coach and manage the school's under-14 team. And working for three months, two sessions a week, with nine- and ten-year-olds at a school near Preston, Lancashire, at the insistence of Percy Jones, a physical education organiser with a reputation second to none. Jones wanted to ensure that when I led a course in soccer for his teachers, I knew what I was talking about. The "professionals" in soccer sometimes accuse the physical educationists of being overly academic. Yet here was the adacemic demanding that the professional truly be so.

Finally, I recall with fondness all the joyful, inspirational, humbling, frustrating, yet satisfying hours I have spent working with players and coaches, at all levels, to make soccer the most enjoyable experience it can be through the development of better skills. It has been a privilege to help players improve both as individuals and as team members. Having played professional soccer, having made most of the mistakes there are to make, yet remaining constant in my belief that soccer is the greatest game in the world, has given me the inspiration and determination to write this book.

INTRODUCTION

How to use this book

The purpose of this book is to help young soccer players improve their ability to play the world's greatest team game. With that in mind, it is aimed at these three groups:

1. **Young players themselves**

2. **Enthusiastic adults** – usually Dads – or Mums

3. **Youth team coaches**

These three groups of people are not separate; indeed, they are sometimes one and the same. Not that a young player can be Dad! But Dad can be – and often is – the team coach.

But while this book is for all of these soccer enthusiasts, each group should approach it in a different way.

Young players

Should concentrate on the first section of Chapters 1 to 12. They should note, too, that Chapters 5 and 9 are set out differently and here, proceed accordingly. Don't worry about the Coaches' Segment at the back of the book.

Each chapter is concerned with one specific skill or aspect of the game: shooting, heading, short passing, goalkeeping, etc. Section I of each chapter will describe the way to execute the particular skill and then give examples of simple yet appropriate practices which a player can do on his own or with a friend. Each practice should be fun and at the same time, have a target to give the young player information that will help him measure his improvement.

Section II of each chapter is aimed particularly at Mum and Dad – the Parent/Coach – should they want to lend a hand in setting up meaning-

15

ful soccer practices, even when only a small group gets together for an informal kick-around.

While there is no need for the young player to read this section, particularly when using the book for the first time to quickly get ideas about how to practise, his enthusiasm for the game should increase as he improves and then he will want to know more. In that way the book becomes something more than a simple coaching ideas manual; it becomes a reference book to be used whenever the need arises.

Even though Section I is fairly straightforward, it should be read very carefully and the illustrations examined closely. Don't be reluctant to read certain parts again and again – especially after practice or a team game when, perhaps, things did not go too well. By studying the text and illustrations, the player will soon develop the ability to analyse his own faults – and put them right.

Enthusiastic adults

I've suggested earlier that this often means Mums or Dads. It is so often the case that the opportunity to help a small group of youngsters, or just one player, arises on the spur of the moment: "Dad. Will you help Scott and Dave and me practise our heading?"

The request has come. The desire to learn and to improve is there. And if you have no other pressing commitments, how can you refuse? But what do you do? It is all in Section II of each chapter. But you should also read Section I so that you can brush up on the facts (if you already know them) and if you don't, you can make sure that you understand the mechanics of executing, say, a defensive header or a push-pass.

And for all of you enthusiastic adults, I would suggest that, prior to reading Sections I and II of the skill chapters, you also read at least the introductory part of the Coaches' Segment. I hope that this in turn will encourage you to look at those parts of the Coaches' Segment that deal with organisation of practices and facilities and equipment. These show how, by simple improvisation, you can mark out realistic practice areas including either goals or targets of some kind.

Youth team coaches

One of the most difficult tasks for coaches in amateur soccer is the organisation and conducting of the team practice session. Not only will numbers vary anything from eight to 28, but you can guarantee that there will still never be the same numbers at two practice sessions running! You can also be quite sure that if a certain practice is to be conducted in two's or four's, there will be odd numbers!

The problem of sustaining interest and enthusiasm while still practising in meaningful situations is always present and you will ignore it at your peril! As well, there are always individuals who need specific attention within the team practice. The goalkeepers are an obvious example!

The all-important, yet basic practices shown in Sections I and II of each chapter will need further developing for your purposes so that they become more relevant to the team practice where combined play is one of the keys to success. Chapters 10, 11 and 12 look specifically at this area of co-operation and understanding between players.

Section III of each chapter sets out to help the coach overcome the team session difficulties, and suggests numerous ways and means to help the session run smoothly, purposefully and enjoyably. However, it is critically important that you first read and understand the whole of the Coaches' Segment (pages 256-300).

Having read this once through thoroughly, you should select those skills or aspects of play you intend to cover, and refresh your knowledge of the fundamentals involved, by reading Section I of the relevant chapter. Then read or flip through Section II to see which of the practices and suggestions will be appropriate to the team practice. Finally, read Section III.

Chapter 1
THE PUSH PASS

 **SECTION I**

In the soccer world, passing with the side of the foot is called the "push-pass" or side foot pass because of the way it is executed. It is the most frequently used method of passing in the game, very accurate up to distances of 10 to 20 yards, and not a difficult technique to master. Over longer distances, it is difficult to provide the power necessary to carry the ball quickly over the surface, and so the push-pass can easily be intercepted. Since most passes in the game are over distances less than 20 yards, you can see how invaluable this particular skill is.

Note, in *illustrations 1, 2 and 3*, the position that the player takes up to enable him to make a successful pass. This perfect stance will vary slightly with each player depending on his height, the length of his legs, and other physical features, but use the illustrations as your model. The non-kicking foot is placed alongside the ball three to six inches away, with the toes of the non-kicking foot pointing in the direction of the intended pass. The striking foot is turned out so it can be used in

1   2   3

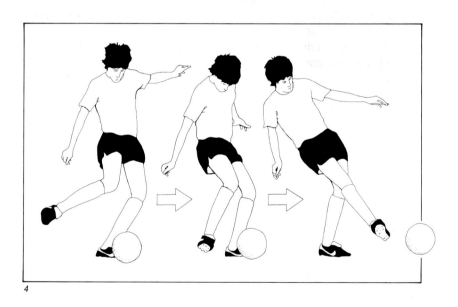

4

much the same manner as an ice hockey stick or golf putter. The balancing non-kicking leg is slightly flexed at the knee. The head is looking down and steady – remember that the golden rule is to keep the eye on the ball. There is no need to worry about the placement of the arms as they will naturally assume a comfortable, balanced position. The body as a whole tends to be wrapping itself over the ball at the moment of impact.

Illustration 4 shows the player performing the pass. Only a limited backswing with his kicking foot is needed as the power comes from "pushing the foot through the ball". Similarly, there is a limited follow-through, always in the direction that the player wishes the ball to go. Because the foot is turned out, it becomes physically impossible to have much of a backswing or follow-through anyway.

Study the position of the head from start to finish. If the head is loose or comes up too early, the pass will be loose. The main objective is to skim the ball across the surface of the field. It should not bobble or come off the ground more than an inch or two as it glides towards the receiver of the pass.

Practice 1

First find a flat rebound surface that can withstand the impact of a soccer ball, or you might find yourself on the wrong end of a telling-off. Garage and school gymnasium walls are good choices, particularly if they are made of concrete.

Begin by just playing the ball off a rebound surface, controlling it and pushing the ball back onto the wall, as shown in *illustration 5*. Once comfortable you can then progress the practice. As you can see, a line has been drawn approximately six yards from the wall.

5

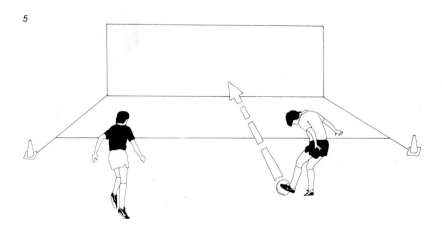

The picture shows two friends practising together but the exercise is just as effective on your own. The rules are that you cannot enter the "no-man's-land" between the line and the wall. You are allowed a maximum of two touches between each pass. In other words, you can control the ball as it comes off the wall and over the line, and so set up the ball for the second touch which must be the pass back onto the wall again. Alternatively, you may eliminate the controlling touch by playing the ball back to the wall as soon as it comes over the line (called "one-touch"). The idea is to keep the practice going for as long as possible without needing three touches, without misdirecting a pass and without the ball failing to return from the no-man's-land area.

Always keep track of your record so that you can see your improvement as well as have a target to beat each practice. As you progress, increase the challenge by timing yourself with a stopwatch. Set the timer, then see how long it takes you to complete 10, or perhaps 20, passes. With two of you, work one and then rest one, or set your "doubles" record together.

Practice 2

In *illustration 6*, the practice has been modified to encourage greater accuracy in passing. Three targets have been marked at the base of the wall with a piece of chalk. As in Practice 1, you cannot enter no-man's-land, and once again it is two-touch maximum. Your targets here can be to score as many hits as possible before the practice breaks down, or count the number of hits you can make in two minutes, or time how long it takes you to make 10 hits.

The rules I have suggested are not hard and fast. You may want to develop your own, or maybe the practice area available to you will be a little different from the one I have illustrated. Don't worry about that. Use your own initiative. **But do not cheat yourself**. Once you have

6

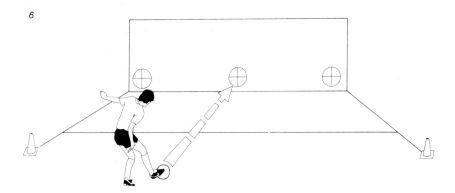

established the rules, abide by them. Otherwise, your "records" won't mean a thing and you will only be fooling yourself.

Practising on your own with a rebound wall is a first-class way to improve your technique, and Practices 1 and 2 can both be performed in this manner. As well, you can work on them with a friend by taking turns first, then competing against each other, either in "totals"or in times.

7

Practice 3

Here we have further development of the wall practice as shown in *illustration 7*, where a game of "soccer squash" has been devised. The rules remain basically the same as in Practices 1 and 2: a two-touch maximum, the ball must return over the line, and it must stay inside the area marked by the cones to be valid. The idea is to "force" an error from your opponent and so score a point. Although in soccer your aim is to find a team mate with a pass, this "soccer squash" game still has enormous benefits, as you need to be very accurate and impart as much pace on the ball as possible to force your opponent's error. Using a table-tennis method of scoring i.e., 21 points to win the game, each player takes a turn in starting the practice (the "service") for five points, then passes the service on to his opponent for a further five, and so on. Also set a height limit – ideally knee-height (see illustration).

As an alternative, work with your friend as a partnership. In this case, you take turns playing the ball against the wall to establish a record of consecutive passes before the practice breaks down. As the partnership becomes more proficient, start competing against the clock. How quickly can you complete 20 consecutive passes between you? Use your stopwatch, set your record and then try to beat it.

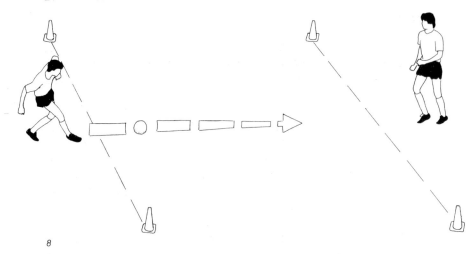

8

9

Practice 4

Illustration 8 shows how you can practise with your friend without having to worry about a rebound surface. Begin by marking two lines of chalk, cones, bricks or what have you – approximately eight to 10 yards apart. The exact distance will depend on your age and ability; the younger you are, the closer you should be. As in the previous practices, the area between the lines becomes no-man's-land. Start informally by playing the ball to your friend and back to you, with two-touch, to get a feel for the practice and to work on good quality passing. You need to really be on your toes: not every pass will be perfect and it is only your alertness that can turn a poor pass into a good one. Once you feel that your passing has improved, put yourselves to the test. The two of you can practise together to establish a record and then, in subsequent attempts, try to top it. The object is to get as many consecutive passes as possible before the practice breaks down and the sequence is finished. This happens if the ball goes out of bounds, stays in no-man's-land, one player touches the ball more than twice, or it is missed by the receiving player.

The alternative method of scoring on this practice is to use the stop-watch again, timing how long it takes you to successfully complete 20 passes, and then trying to better your performance.

Practice 5

Practice 5 is a development of Practice 4, but now two players compete against one another. As *illustration 9* indicates, a goal is established by the use of cones – or whatever other markers are available – placed in the middle of no-man's-land and approximately two yards apart. The object is to pass the ball between the posts to score a point. Other markers are used to set the limits of the lines; lines are some 10 yards wide, and the posts are positioned opposite one another. The distance across no-man's-land again can vary from eight to 10 yards. A decision must be made as to who starts the practice; from then on, it is started by the non-erring player of the previous point as there is an obvious advantage in beginning the practice with a static ball.

The starting position sees the ball placed on the ground facing the goal. The two-touch rule applies and the practice continues until a mistake is made. That means a whole series of goals or points can be scored in one sequence. Actually hitting one of the two goalposts does not score a goal nor does it count as an error. It is considered a "near miss" and the player who struck the post must restart the practice by rolling the ball across to the other player. No points count on a "roll". In all other circumstances, as long as the ball is passing out of no-man's-land and between the markers, the action continues. Should a pass be played outside the cones marking the no-man's-land, the non-erring player is given the opportunity of starting from a static ball position, and is able to score right away by a foot pass – not a roll. This practice calls for exceptionally accurate passing and first-class ball control.

Those are some simple exercises that you youngsters can go away and work on. But you don't have to practise the push-pass for the next hour, or even 20 minutes. Five minutes may be plenty. "Little and often" is the key. Enjoy working together to set records, but don't be afraid of those sessions when you actually compete against one another.

And now let's review the basics of the all-important push-pass. Non-kicking foot placed alongside the ball. Kicking foot turned out. Short backswing and follow-through in the direction you want the ball to go, using a sweeping movement. Keep the head steady and looking at the ball. Strike through the centre of the ball with the kicking foot slightly raised off the ground, and try to skim the ball across the surface without any bouncing. As you can see in *illustration 10*, the actual striking part of the turned out foot will be nearer the heel than the toe as this is the largest striking area, and transmits the solid power from the leg and the swing. Don't forget to use both feet – right and left, left and right.

10

⚽ ⚽ SECTION II

Youngsters love to experiment on their own but they also like to be organised. Helping set up practices for a small group of young players gives them an opportunity for both. **Always** finish with some form of game which is as close as possible – in spite of the numbers – to the real thing.

The practices described in Section I should be easily understood by youngsters but if they are having some difficulty, give them a helping hand so they know what to do on their own in future. These practices are not "kids' stuff": the importance of acquiring the basic skills – the techniques of the game – cannot be stressed too vigorously. If you can't pass the ball in soccer, **you can't play**. The legendary manager of the great Liverpool team of the 1960s and '70s, Scotsman Bill Shankly, always maintained that "the giving and taking of passes were the essence of footba'". In non-Scottish, layman's terms, what Shankly meant was that passing and ball control (the taking of passes) are the two most valuable basic skills of the game. The majority of soccer authorities would endorse Bill Shankly's remarks.

Practice 6

Work with a group of four or more in pairs, with lines separating them as described in Practice 4 (see *illustration 11*). Start by allowing some non-stressful practice time with the ball going backwards and forwards. If there are obvious faults, offer useful tips but do ask for quality work. Always encourage players to use both feet; you might even modify the practice for a period of time so that they must use the right and left foot alternately. Once the practice is operating smoothly, pairs can begin competing against one another. Which will be the first pair to successfully complete 20 consecutive passes? Or how many passes can a pair complete in one minute? The coach keeps a check on the time and supervises the practice to make sure there is no cheating.

Practice 7

A soccer veteran, Ron Moran, once told me that they spoiled the game when they introduced opposition – until then, he claimed, it had been relatively easy. It was an amusing remark but there is much in what he said. Sooner or later, opponents must be put into a practice to provide the essential ingredients of realism.

In *illustration 12*, a square area has been set up – anything from eight to 12 yards per side, depending on players' age and ability – for a two

11

12

versus one or a three versus one game. Even four versus one in a 15-yard square is a good way to start. The presence of an opponent demands quality play to prevent the practice from breaking down. The one opponent is encouraged to do everything possible to force the error or to win the ball in the tackle. The simple objective of the two, three or four attackers is to keep the ball away from the "defender" and in the playing area. The attackers will need to rely on co-operation and a great deal of passing, mostly employing the push-pass technique. The coach can stimulate the competition by setting targets encouraging players to "try to get six consecutive passes".

The coach should change the players around so they can all try defending. If two versus one works best at a given time yet there are four or five players, don't be afraid to temporarily leave one or two on the sidelines. This type of practice is hard work, so the opportunity to take a rest will be well received. You might introduce the two-touch rule described in Section I of this chapter but I would not advise it just yet. Even top professionals would have difficulty with two versus one in a 10-yard square if the two-touch rule were applied. It is more important that players feel comfortable with the practice and with the ball at their feet and not be under too much pressure to play the ball off quickly. When a player is uncertain about making a pass, he should "screen" the ball away from the opponent until the right opportunity to pass to a team mate presents itself (see Chapter 6, Dribbling or Running with the Ball, regarding screening).

Practice 8

The ability to keep the ball, to maintain possession as in Practice 7, so that the opposition is denied the opportunity to attack is of fundamental importance in soccer. **But it cannot be an end in itself**. Sooner or later, progress has to be made down the field to reach the striking area. The game is about goals, and all practices must have in mind that the ultimate objective is both to score goals and to prevent the opposition from scoring goals.

Illustration 13 shows a simple two versus two being played in a 10 x 20 yard field, with improvised goals (two yards in width, using cones or corner flags) at both ends. The rules are modified to accommodate the circumstances. No goalkeepers and no handling. Goals will only count if they are below knee-height. Kick-ins replace throw-ins because of the small size of the field. No offsides. In all other respects, the normal rules of the game apply.

This game is excellent practice in short-passing and in "combining" with a team mate. It also provides the enjoyment of playing the game, the point I stressed earlier. It is preferable that any type of practice session finishes with a game.

If there are only three young players, then Dad or whoever is taking the practice can make up the teams. If there are five, do the same and play three versus three in a bigger area. Even a one versus one game, if there are only two players, is an enjoyable way to finish – but extremely hard work, so five to 10 minutes will be ample. Or use Practice 2 in Chapter 3 on Shooting – called "three-goals-in" – as another game for two or three to finish a practice session.

SECTION III

Undoubtedly the most difficult aspect of coaching is that of organising the team practice, particularly when dealing with numbers which can often range from a handful of players to as many as 20 or 30. Dividing them into groups of the right numbers and setting up appropriate practice areas are dealt with elsewhere in the book. The practices in the push-pass described in Sections I and II of this chapter can all be adapted to the team practice – some more readily than others. Remember it is vitally important to maintain the interest and enthusiasm of the players through the right mix of drills and small-sided games. And don't attempt too much in one session.

Practice 9

In this practice we have a circle of players (*illustration 14*). The numbers can vary from six to 12, although you must consider that the greater the numbers, the fewer kicks per person! With 12 players, it may be better to work in two groups; eight or nine per group is probably just right. One player stands in the middle of the circle, and the object is to keep the ball away from him by passing. It is for the coach to decide just how big the circle will be and then ensure that it does not drift outwards. The marked centre circle of a soccer field can be used to control the group. The bigger the circle, the easier it is to maintain possession – and the more difficult it is for the man in the middle to win the ball. The coach may, if he wishes, condition the practice to two-touch or one-touch but it probably won't be necessary, as any player taking more than two touches will give the middle man a good chance of tackling for the ball. After a misplaced pass or an interception, the man in the middle changes places with the erring outside player. One further rule is that the first pass is free – that is, it cannot be intercepted. This is necessary to enable the practice to get under way.

It is sometimes debatable just who the major offender is when a pass

13

14

is intercepted; in such cases a decision will have to be made either by the coach or by democratic method. This is an excellent warm-up passing activity, popular with soccer players around the world. The coach can also leave the group to enjoy this activity while he sets up areas for another practice.

Practice 10

This simple drill (*illustration 15*) is a fine way to practice good passing, principally with the side of the foot. An ideal number of players for this practice is six to eight so you may need to work with more than one group. Two files of players face one another, and a distance is set and maintained between the two files – about 10 yards if you're concentrating on the push-pass, seven to eight yards for younger players. The object is to play the ball to the player opposite and then run (or sprint if fully warmed up) to the back of the opposite file. The coach can encourage – even stipulate – that the pass be to the left or the right foot. Initially the condition can be two-touch but as players become proficient and, just as importantly, warmed up, it can be changed to one-touch. Obviously with one-touch, the whole speed of the practice increases, almost compelling players to sprint after each pass in order to get to the back of the opposite file in time for the next one. Alternatively (*illustration 16*) players can use the one-touch rule to play the ball and move to the back of their own file.

15

16

Practice 11

This is an exercise that the coach can adapt for a number of different situations and skills. Players pair off with a ball between them and are confined to a marked area as shown in *illustration 17*. If there are odd numbers, have one group of three. The coach tells the pairs to inter-pass while they have the freedom to move anywhere within the area. Obviously the players, although working in pairs, have to be very aware of other players or there will be physical clashes as well as passes going astray through hitting moving bodies. It serves as an excellent preparation for a more formalised situation (see Practice 12), bringing in the important factors of movement and judgement. The accuracy and speed of the pass must coincide with the run of the partner. The coach can make the practice really live by regularly throwing in such instructions as, "play a one-two," "turn and sprint away for five yards after you make your pass," or "move off in a different direction when you receive the ball and keep it under close control".

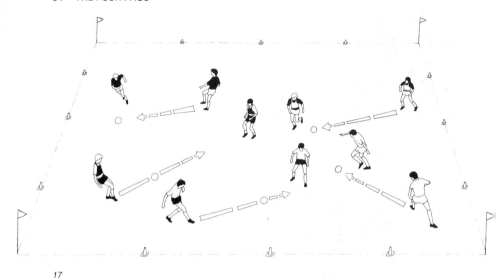

17

Practice 12

This is a four versus two practice in an area 20 yards square (see *illustration 18*). The object is for the four to keep possession away from the two – an extension of Practice 7, dealt with in Section II of this chapter. Eight players practise in each 20-yard area, but if you are working with odd numbers, you can easily use three versus one or five versus two as well as the main four versus two's. Players compete to see which group of four can get the most consecutive passes before the ball goes out of play, or is intercepted or won by the two defenders.

As two defend, two rest, and after a period of time – say, two minutes – they change with their team mates who then have their rest. Obviously, the four attackers don't have a rest at this stage but they have the advantage of numbers anyway. The two defenders should be the ones who are working hardest chasing around in an attempt to get the ball. When a mistake is made, the sequence of passes finishes and the practice is restarted by one of the four attackers playing the ball. Then the defenders get their turn as attackers. The two defending pairs join forces to become four, and the former attackers split into two pairs to defend, with each pair having a rest period. It may well be that you cover Practice 7 (two versus one and three versus one) before moving onto this practice, but it is by no means essential.

Coaches should not get the impression that the only way to develop practices is to progress them by increasing the numbers. Although it is logical to go from pairs practice without opposition to two versus

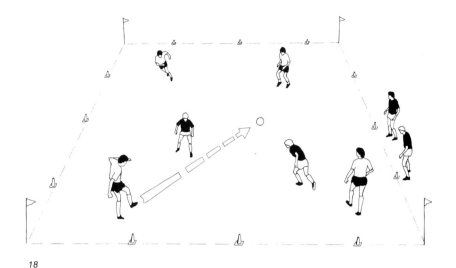

18

one's, to three versus one's, to four versus two's, and so on, it is up to each coach to decide what he thinks is the most suitable practice for his group of players. Bear in mind that to go through the whole range of number progressions of a particular skill will mean a series of reorganisational time-outs that **could be boring to young players**.

Remember there are many practices other than those mentioned here. Review the Coaches' Segment once again, then using my suggestions, you can adapt some of the practices shown in this chapter or devise your own, to suit the specific needs of your team.

Practice 13

Illustration 19 (on page 36) shows a three versus three small-sided game using the "change-soccer" method. You can see the field has been marked out with small goals; dimensions are 30 x 20 yards here but can be varied to suit the age and ability of the players. This practice, like so many others in the book, is ideally suited to both the indoor and the outdoor session. The three versus three proceeds in a normal way with throw-ins, goal kicks, and corners. The other players on each goal-line are the goalkeepers, and link up to form a goalkeeping wall. Goals can only be scored below knee-height. Because goalkeepers cannot handle the ball, they must move as a block to prevent a goal from being scored. Also they cannot move more than three yards out of the goal. A goal approximately three to four yards wide would be appropriate.

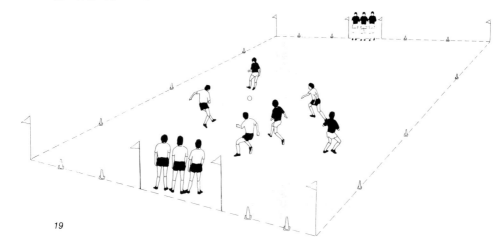

19

The coach can shout "change" at any time, at which signal the out-field players must leave the ball immediately and take up position as the goalkeepers. At the very same time, the goalkeepers move out as quickly as possible to continue the game as outfielders before the oppositon can gain an advantage. Besides being fun and competitive, the game allows youngsters to improve their passing and appreciate the value of co-operation with others in forming an effective "team effort".

The small-sided game can be adapted, in terms of numbers and field dimensions, to accommodate smaller or larger groups. In this particular practice, 12 players are involved, but you can work with groups of 10 to 16 simply by using four versus four or two versus two, possibly in combination with a three versus three. Don't be afraid of odd or awk-ward numbers, even if it takes a little longer to organise and set the rules. Use Practice 9 as the "fall-back position" while you take time to work out the combinations. **Remember you can always join in if it solves the number problem**. Even if you are not a great soccer player, you can gain respect by your willingness and enthusiasm. If you are a good soccer player, join the weaker team!

The advantage of having the players not directly involved in the three versus three as goalkeepers is twofold:

1.   Although not as involved as the outfield players, they are still an important part of the team and their performance as goalkeepers will help determine their team's success.
2.   Their skill in defending the goal as a wall is a good introduction to the defensive wall circumstance necessary when defending against some free kicks.

Chapter 2
THE FRONT OF THE FOOT PASS

 **SECTION I**

In Chapter 1, we deal with the simple, accurate and effective push-pass. Now, let's look at the more exciting and challenging methods of striking a soccer ball with the front of the foot – the instep – or, as some old pros refer to it, "kicking with the laces".

The ability to control the ball, look up, see one's team mates in different positions and pass to them is a wonderful asset in soccer. Consider the successful player's repertoire of skills: he can drive a pass straight as an arrow to a player 40 yards away; chip the ball over defenders into the path of a forward-running team mate; fire a 60-yard lofted pass into attacking areas of the field or switch the play from one side of the field to the other with a brilliant raking pass. But, of course, to achieve that level of competence requires practice – and plenty of it.

The low drive

The "low drive", as the name suggests, is a driven pass or shot staying close to the ground that needs to move quickly to its target – a team mate or the opponent's goal. Note, in *illustation 20*, the body position just prior to striking the ball. The head is looking down – eye on the ball – and steady. The body is wrapping itself over the ball, but also leaning slightly away to allow the kicking leg to swing through the action – powerfully, and without running the risk of stubbing the toe in the turf. It is essential that the kicking foot points downwards so that the front of the foot – the shoelaces – becomes the hammerhead that strikes the ball on its course (*illustration 21*). The foot is locked at the ankle on impact, and the ball is struck around the centre or a little below. The non-kicking foot is placed alongside the ball approximately six to eight inches away at the moment of striking the ball.

Study the illustration showing the movements leading up to the pass. The low drive requires a much bigger backswing than the side foot

20

21

22

23

pass does and, as well, a greater follow-through after impact (*illustration 22*). The importance of the follow-through should not be under-estimated: when the follow-through is executed in the direction of the intended pass, the ball is "beamed" almost radar-like on its way to the target. Never lean back, or even stand upright, when kicking the ball as this will cause the pass to be lofted.

24

The lofted pass

Because a pass may be intercepted by the opposition or to propel the ball over long distances, the "lofted pass" becomes a crucial skill to acquire and practise. In execution it is almost identical to the low drive except that the non-kicking foot is placed slightly behind the ball and a little further to the side.

As well, the body leans a little more away from the ball (see *illustration 23*). The distance a player can kick the ball will vary with his age, strength and physique, and practice of the lofted drive will allow a player to find out his range.

The illustration (*24*) demonstrates proper technique. All the key points mentioned in the description of the low drive must also be observed here: head down and steady, eye on the ball. Kicking foot locked on impact, toes pointing downwards. Follow through in direction of intended pass. But to give the desired height, the impact point on the ball is equally critical. With the lofted drive, the ball should be struck at the lower half – the lower the strike, the greater the height.

Swerved passes and shots

To deliberately swerve a ball in order to bamboozle a defence or perhaps a goalkeeper, variations of the lofted and low drive techniques are
needed. Modifying the body position can swerve the ball, as can follow-
through, striking the ball off its centre-line and off the centre-line of the
instep, or a combination of these methods. Swerved passes are fun to
practise and very effective at the right time in a game. However, I believe
that players must first perfect the basic passes so that the ball can be
hit firmly and accurately. The sophistications of bending the ball can be
developed once the basics are mastered.

25   26

Chipped pass

This is an important technique and a variation on the lofted drive (see
illustration 26). It requires less of a backswing and less of a follow-
through than other passes, giving it something of a stubbing action

27

(see *illustration 27*). The underside of the ball is struck to give the pass its height (see *illustration 25*). This action also imparts backspin to the ball, slowing it down and so minimising its forward movement when it hits the ground. The backspin does make it a little more difficult to control the ball as it will tend to spin off and away from the controlling part of the player's body, particularly when receiving the ball with his back towards the goal. Greater elevation to the pass can be obtained by kicking the ball in front of the non-kicking foot and by leaning back more. The chipped pass is an exciting and effective pass that warrants plenty of practice.

Flick pass

The flick pass is much in evidence at the top levels of the game. As you see from the *illustration 28* it is an efficient way of passing while running with the ball, particularly when confronted by an opponent. It can be executed quickly, with little or no preparation, as the player is on his run: the foot strikes sharply – snake-like – at the ball, and no backswing or change of position are needed. The ball is kicked as the player strides forward, so a decision can be made and the pass carried out rapidly with no early warning given to the opponent.

Compare the flick pass with the side foot pass. The side foot pass requires an elaborate movement of the body to shape up for the pass. This takes time and worse, gives the opposition plenty of clues as to what will happen next. The flick pass makes use of the front of the foot,

28

29

but inclines more to the outside of the instep (as in *illustration 29*), particularly when an opponent is involved: the ball is normally struck *off* the centre-line of both the laces and the ball itself to direct it away from the challenging opponent.

Look again at *illustrations 30 and 31* to see a most effective application of the flick pass. The outside player has made a forward run to help his team mate who is confronted by a defender. It is extremely difficult for an opponent to "read" the flick pass as there are virtually no early clues that it is going to be used. The flick technique would also be useful in a situation when a player was confronted by an advancing

30

31

keeper on a run through to goal. In this case, the flick could be used to steer the ball away from the keeper and into the goal. (See Shooting, Chapter 3.)

One important word of caution, though. The flick pass is a valuable pass *but it requires great touch to get the right accuracy and the right power*. Most *young* players using it would unfortunately have a high failure rate.

Volley practice

Volleying the ball is an essential technique requiring great timing and accuracy. A volley pass or clearance takes place when a ball is in the air from a lofted pass, clearance or header, and is struck before it is controlled and before it hits the ground. It is a fundamental skill as mis-hits often result in lost goals in defending areas and lost scoring opportunities in the attacking penalty area. The circumstances necessitating volleying vary considerably – a crossed ball, lofted passes, headed clearances – but they can easily be practised by using a thrown service to simulate game situations. You can even throw or bounce the ball on your own to present the volleying opportunity. (Volleying for goal will be covered in detail in Chapter 3.)

The low drive, the lofted pass and the chipped pass are the most important front of the foot passes to practise, and this is where I believe the main emphasis should be. Once you have mastered them, you will have little difficulty in adding the subtleties of such variations as the flick and swerve. Volleying will require repeated practice.

32

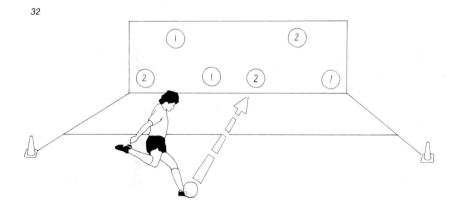

Practice 1

To practise on your own, return to your trusty rebound wall. (See Chapter 1, Practice 1.) Using targets marked on the wall – good soccer players always have a piece of chalk! – and with a line indicating the limit from where you can make the pass, devise you own game to test your accuracy using the low drive technique. For instance, you might count the number of hits you make on the targets with, say, 20 passes. Or you can divide the target into areas with two points for the main targets and one point for the adjacent area (see *illustration 32*).

Remember to practise with *both* feet. Don't use a stationary ball. Touch the ball to the side and then strike the pass. As you improve, try to keep a sequence going – two-touches maximum – where the ball must return over the marking line before you can control it (one touch) and then strike at the target (the second touch).

33

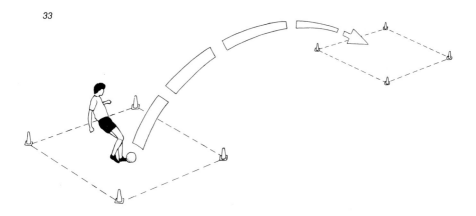

Practice 2

Still on your own, find an area of reasonable size and be prepared to do a little jogging while you practise your lofted and chipped passes.

In *illustration 33*, a starting area (as shown by the square) is set some distance from the vicinity of the target. You can decide, by trial and error, the best distances for yourself, and that will depend on which skill you are practising – nearer for the chipped pass, farther away for the lofted pass.

Start off soccer-style, rather than just rolling the ball forward. For instance, throw the ball several feet in the air, control it when it comes down and then hit the pass. If necessary, have another touch of the ball with the foot to set up a good position to hit your pass into the target area. Having access to a soccer field will allow you to utilise existing markings such as the centre circle and goal area in your practice. And if you have more than one ball to practise with, so much the better. Don't forget to use both feet. You can have some good fun practising chipping with all sorts of targets – even a dustbin. But whether it's the practice in *illustration 33* or the dustbin, keep track of your record – e.g., 20 passes, 9 successes – and strive for constant improvement.

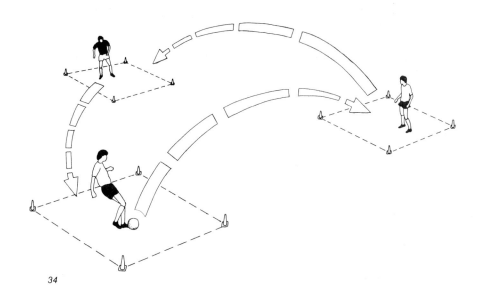

34

Practice 3

With friends, it is easy to set up a practice similar to Practice 2 for either the chipped or lofted pass, using the target areas as the position for each player (*illustration 34*). Set the rules and after a period of relaxed practice, make it more purposeful and competitive.

Working together, see how many successful consecutive passes you can make where the ball must bounce first time in the target areas. The receiver has three touches maximum after the ball bounces. Even though the ball may have to be controlled outside the area after the bounce, it must be brought back into the area for the pass – but remember, it is three touches maximum.

You can also compete against each other, counting the number of successful passes individually. Here you need to decide how to restart the practice after a wayward pass. One suggestion is to throw the ball in the air 10 feet, control and then pass towards the next target.

Remember to work on both the right and left foot. You may well make one part of the practice "left foot only" or "right foot only". You should also consider going clockwise and anti-clockwise if there are three or more of you practising, as in *illustration 34*.

🏐🏐 SECTION II

The suggestions made in Section I should enable young players to organise themselves, but we all respond better to direction – especially if the coach can make things stimulating. So the parent/coach should help and encourage youngsters to practise. When the initial interest begins to wane, inspire them by setting new objectives – or decide it's time to move into more of a game situation.

Practice 4

"Pig-in-the-middle" (*illustration 35*) is half practice, half game. And if there are only two young players, you may have to be the "pig", if you'll excuse the expression.

The object is to pass the ball from one outside square to the other without the pig intercepting, making sure at the same time that the ball doesn't come out of the end squares – even after the player in the square controls it. Three touches maximum is a good rule to impose (two-touch may be too difficult at this stage) and the method of passing is decided by the individual.

Vary the distance between the end squares according to the age and ability of the players, and the type of pass you wish to encourage. With 10 yards separating the end squares, as in the illustration, the two most

35

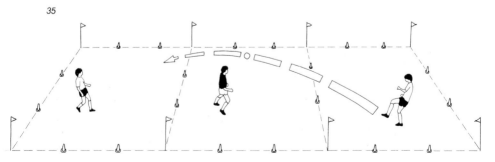

effective passes will be the low drive and the chipped. A greater distance between the end squares – say 30 yards – will bring in the lofted pass. Modify the rules as you see fit. For example, when a mistake is made, the offending player might change with the man in the middle. Or with large numbers – say four or five – develop a sequence whereby the offending end player takes a rest, the pig takes his position, and the outside player comes into the middle, and so on. With five or even four, you can always put two pigs in the middle and maybe widen the area by a few yards. If there are six or more, set up two practice areas.

Practice 5

In adaptation of the previous practice, distances in length and width have been increased to encourage the use of the lofted pass. As you can see in *illustration 36*, two pigs-in-the-middle work together, with one player going to the rear of the central section while the other applies pressure from the front of the same section. Dad may have to adjust the practice area dimensions as young players become more competent.

Keep score of how many successful sequences players achieve before an interception or an error. Emphasise the use of both feet and if necessary, make it a rule. Besides being enjoyable, this is a very realistic and effective passing practice.

36

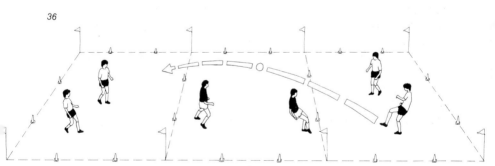

Practice 6

Back to the low drive again. As *illustration 37* shows, two lines are drawn approximately 20 to 25 yards apart and a cone is set up as a centre target. The object is to hit the target.

Start with free practice as the situation is competitive enough without establishing too many rules and conditions. However, as the

37

youngsters improve, set up a challenge – either one player versus another or one pair versus another – to see how many hits can be made in 20 passes. This practice can be specifically related to ball control by your insisting on two-touch (see Chapter 8, Controlling the Ball), which will also make it a more realistic exercise. After a direct hit or a misdirected pass, restart by touching the ball to one side and then passing.

SECTION III

Refresh your "ideas bank" by reviewing the practices in Sections I and II. All can be used in the team practice, but need to be carefully organised and planned for because of the "numbers" complication you will face. Eventually, you can progress to the more involved teamwork of Practices 7 and 8, but don't be in too much of a hurry. You will do perfectly well just by sticking to the earlier practices, and working up to five-or six-a-side games. The following practices are exciting but do require careful organisation and *good skill level.*

Practice 7

This is a further development of the pig-in-the-middle practice but using greater numbers to accommodate the team squad (see *illustration 38*). Split the youngsters into three groups of three or whatever number is practical. The dimensions of the practice area are only approximate and should be adjusted according to the age and ability of the players. The purpose of the practice is to keep possession (three versus one) in each end section, but to try to pass out of one end section to the other. If success is not forthcoming, take out the defender in the central section. You might also increase the dimensions of the practice area – or use both methods. Flexibility is your tool so don't be afraid of adjusting the practice or practice area to make things work.

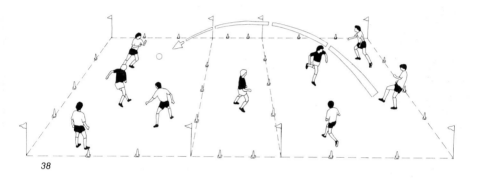

38

To avoid complaints such as "our trio did well, it was your group's poor passing", judge success by the defending group. The three with the least number of successful passes against are the winners. Or if you are a real mathematical whizkid you can add each group's successful passes, then subtract all passes accumulated against them when defending.

Don't be put off by this practice just because you have numbers other than nine. Keep juggling. For example, try three groups of four players, giving a four versus one but with two players in the middle.

Practice 8

Illustration 39 shows a development of the previous practice into a more realistic situation with the opportunity to score goals – very important!

You can see that the practice has been split up into thirds. The dimensions given are only a guideline and will vary according to

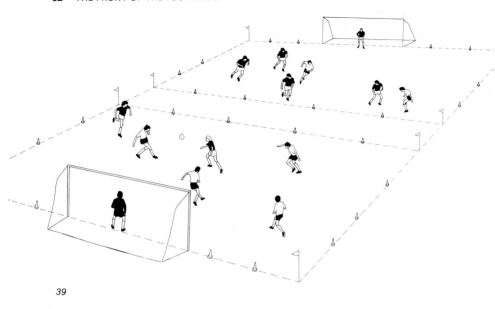

39

players' age, and ability, and the numbers you have to work with. Two goalkeepers, four versus two and four versus two are indicated, but it doesn't have to be that way.

The defence is overloaded to enable it to maintain possession and to have time to look up to make the forward pass to the two attackers. The attackers, although heavily outnumbered, have a fighting chance of gaining possession and striking for goal, particularly if good accurate passes are played out from defence. Remember the purpose of the practice is to concentrate on passing, and incorporate all of them: the short push-pass to maintain possession in the four versus two, and then accurate driven, lofted and chipped balls into the front players' two versus four.

Chapter 3
SHOOTING FOR GOAL

⚉ SECTION I

"If you can't pass, you can't play" summarises what was said in Chapters 1 and 2. But "if you can't score, you can't win" – and that's another simple fact of the game of soccer. The art of finishing is of paramount importance. Passing is the means to the end. You need to be able to pass the ball well to enable the team to enter the **scoring zone**. Naturally, the more times you enter the scoring zone, the greater the chances of successfully striking at goal.

Most goals – over 90 per cent, it has been calculated – are scored from the area that has been shaded in *illustration 40*. For this reason, most shooting drills should have the finishing part of the practice – the shot – taking place in the shaded scoring zone area.

Kicking powerfully and accurately, and kicking not so powerfully but *precisely* are the keys to goal-scoring. Kicking the ball in a skilful manner is the only way to pass properly and score goals – other than by heading, which will be dealt with in Chapter 5. So passing and shooting have *almost* the same techniques. *Almost* because kicking techniques must be modified occasionally due to time constraints and the proximity of challenges, but the same basic methods of striking the ball are employed.

There are different ways of scoring goals but in this chapter, we will concentrate on scoring by kicking, practising shots with the side of the foot, driven shots with the front of the foot, chipped shots, flicked shots away from a goalkeeper and volley shooting.

It is impossible to recommend any one technique as the best to use; different situations will call for different approaches. The circumstances will dictate whether you have time to draw your foot back and power a shot at goal, or whether, under challenge and with the goal-

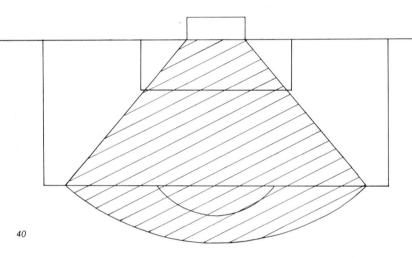

40

41

keeper advancing, the attacking player chooses to flick it wide of the goalkeeper – maybe even toe-poke into goal. Chesting the ball over the goal line from one yard out, with the goalkeeper beaten by the cross, has been exactly the right thing to do in the scoring of some very important goals.

So "the right thing at the right time" can be achieved only through much practice and by experiencing scoring situations similar to match play. When a player feels composed and confident in the scoring zone, he will be able to make the right choice of how to strike for goal.

The following photographs illustrate some of the different striking methods and situations.

Look closely at *illustration 41* which shows a typical scoring opportunity. The striking player is being heavily challenged as he attempts a shot at goal. To compensate for the challenge, he is leaning into and holding off the defender while still maintaining his "shape" to enable him to strike strongly and accurately at goal. Whether a striker is big or small, he must be determined and strong enough not to be easily brushed off the ball.

The striking player in *Illustration 42* has just enough time to employ a full backswing and follow-through. This gives him the opportunity of a powerful strike at goal before the challenging defender is able to close down.

Illustrations 43 and 44 show a simple side foot shot. The attacker has slipped away from his marking defender in order to gain a half yard advantage to meet a ground pass that has been squared across from

42

43

44

45

the side of the penalty area, or possibly pulled back from the goal line. The side foot shot requires great composure and accuracy when contact is made with the ball. The shot is thus steered away from the goalkeeper. A very high percentage of goals scored come from this type of situation.

The attacking player on the edge of the penalty area is shaping up for a chipped shot into the far corner of the goal (*illustration 45*). Because of the number of players between the ball and the goal the chip will give least chance of an interception. What is more, the goalkeeper will almost certainly lose sight of the ball as it travels towards the goal.

Illustrations 46 and 47 show volley shooting where the ball is struck before reaching the ground. Successful volleying requires perfect timing and boldness on the part of the striker, who must also be willing to take the attendant risk of looking foolish through a mishit. Failure to be bold and positive will almost certainly result in a missed opportunity, however, as defenders will then have time to challenge while the attacker tries to control the ball. In *illustration 46*, the striking player has gained a yard advantage on the defender and has moved in quickly to meet a ball crossed from the sides of the penalty box. Note his position as he leans backwards and sideways in order to hit over the top of the ball and so keep it down. Otherwise it would probably sail over the cross bar.

In *illustration 47*, a penalty area clearance – a goalkeeper's punch or a defender's headed clearance – is being met by the shooting player before it hits the ground, and before defenders push out on top of him. The volley shot in this circumstance requires a relaxed strike with a "loose" ankle to cause the ball to dip under the cross bar. Striking the ball too hard will send it high, wide and not-so-handsome.

46

47

48

49

Illustrations 48 and 49 show a player moving towards the six-yard box with a heavy challenge coming in, as well as the goalkeeper advancing. The player flick-shoots – he could even toe-poke the ball – past and away from the goalkeeper. The great advantage of this shot is that it is taken in the stride of the attacking player and so requires no complicated "shaping up". Also, since it gives little warning to the goalkeeper and defender, they are unable to anticipate.

Illustrations 50 and 51 show the attacker faking the defender to move him off the line between the ball and the goal – otherwise the defender would block the shot. Once moved off the line, a shot must be taken quickly; otherwise, the defender is likely to recover.

50

51

Illustrations 52 and 53 demonstrate how the attacker has skilfully and successfully gambled by turning on the defender to make a scoring chance. The gamble is to be encouraged because the rewards are high – a shot, maybe a goal. And the defender must be careful about making a rash challenge, as he will risk conceding a penalty and an almost certain goal.

In contrast to *illustrations 52 and 53* the attacking player in this action shot has elected not to turn himself with the ball (*illustrations 54 and 55*). Instead he has laid off a simple pass to set up a team mate in a more favourable shooting position. Note how the passing player has immediately moved off to seek another attacking position – possibly to look for a rebound from the goalkeeper after a shot goes in.

52

53

54

55

The do's and don'ts of shooting

1. **Don't** strike for goal if an opponent is directly in front of you. Most times he will block the ball.

2. **Do** "fake" an opponent who is blocking the route to goal so that a shooting angle can be opened up. Or move the ball to one side to create a clear strike at goal.

3. **Do** screen the ball away from an opponent as he tries to challenge for it, but at the same time don't allow yourself to be turned away or wide of the goal.

4. **Don't** go for a strong powerful shot if you are about to be challenged from the front. By the time you draw your foot back and begin the long swing for the shot, it will probably be too late and the strike will be blocked.

5. **Do** consider flicking or stabbing the ball at goal if you are under heavy challenge and near to goal, with the goalkeeper advancing. The speed of the action, the element of surprise, defenders' difficulty in "reading" the shot and the accuracy of a controlled flick or toe-poke may just be what you need to produce a goal.

6. **Don't** try to strike the ball too hard when the pass is played to you across the penalty area for a shot. A controlled shot or an accurate "steering" of the ball towards the goal will most times be the best method. The pace desired for the shot will come, in part, from the pass across the penalty area anyway.

7. **Do** look to "power" a shot from the edge of the area if the goalkeeper is in a good position. When a goalkeeper is ready, he should deal with most shots from that distance comfortably, **unless the power and the accuracy leave him no time to make the necessary movements**.

8. **Do** look to see where the goalkeeper is positioned. If there are a number of players grouped between you and the goal in the scoring zone, then a chipped or a swerved shot may catch the opposition by surprise and the goalkeeper unsighted.

9. **Don't** be afraid of volleying a shot for goal, but relax as you strike it. The volley shot is the most difficult one for a goalkeeper to read. It is also probably the most difficult to execute – so practise it. The volley is particularly effective when moving onto a half clearance from a goalkeeper's punch or a defender's headed clearance.

10. **Don't** "pass" the responsibility, if you are in a good scoring position. You will be acting in the best interest of the team and yourself if you have the courage to shoot for goal. However...

11. **Do** consider passing to a better placed team mate who is in or entering the scoring zone if you are outside it, or your own chances of scoring are poor.

12. **Don't** be afraid of attempting to turn to create a scoring position when receiving the ball with your back to goal in the scoring zone. Remember, defenders must be very careful not to commit a foul or they could concede a penalty kick, giving an almost certain goal.

13. **Do** have the courage to take chances in the scoring zone. It's worth considering a dribble past an opponent, an unexpected trick, or a gamble with a volley shot. The risk of failure is always present but the rewards of success are great.

14. **Do** follow up every shot or cross on goal in case the goalkeeper mis-handles or a defender mis-kicks. Always look for the half-chance or the "gift".

Summary

With all these different considerations in shooting, you have to remember that practice makes perfect – and there is no more exciting or enjoyable practice than shooting for goal. Try to simulate the circumstances that produce the different shots described so far.

Practice 1

On your own or with a friend, using a rebound surface, mark a goal and within it, four squares numbered one to four (*illustration 56*). The reason for leaving the middle section blank is that most times, with an able goalkeeper, there is only a limited chance of a goal being scored in the central area. The numbers help in that, on your own, you can pick out the number to hit. With a friend, the number can be shouted out for the other player. Use your imagination. In your mind's eye picture opponents coming in left, right and centre, even use cones as opponents to avoid; and imagine the goalkeeper taking up a good position, maybe even advancing towards you.

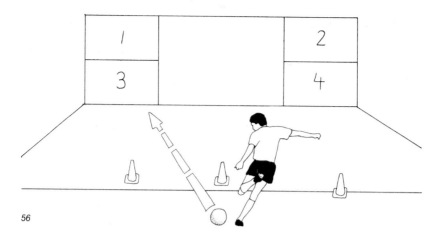

Practice 2
Three-goals-in

In this game, using two cones or markers positioned as in *illustration 57*, the shooter starts in the "D" of the penalty area each time. He can go to the left or right of the cone, or centrally between the cones. Once he plays the ball forward of the cones, however, he must shoot with the next touch. Until then, he can have as many touches as he likes and change directions freely.

A player can shoot anytime and from anywhere in the shaded area of the illustration. He *must* alternate from outside a cone to a central shot between cones on successive shots, but *only on those in advance* of the line beyond the cones. This is to vary the angle of shooting in a more realistic way. The player himself chooses which cone he goes around – right and left – and does not have to alternate the cones. So the sequence is shot from centre, shot from outside of either cone, plus a longer shot at *any time* from behind the cones.

57

The goalkeeper can take up any position he likes. If he is silly enough to gamble on narrowing the angle too early, he will expose himself to the chip shot from behind the cones, as the shooter *does not*, of course, have to go past the cones to shoot. The rule is once *past* the cones, he *must* shoot. When a player has scored three goals, he changes over with the goalkeeper – hence, three-goals-in.

The practice can be made competitive by counting the number of shots needed to score three goals. The player needing the fewest shots for three goals wins. As you can appreciate, this is a good game for practising your goalkeeping, too.

Practice 3
Shooting and defence

"Shooting and defence" (*illustration 58*) can be played with as few as three or as many as six although three or four are the best numbers. One player, the goalkeeper, starts by throwing the ball somewhere around the edge of the penalty area. All outfield players compete against each other. The person who is first to the ball becomes – for that moment, anyway – the attacker looking to get a shot at goal. The others attempt to win the ball for themselves and therefore act as defenders until successfully winning possession, at which stage they become the attackers and attempt to have their own shot at goal. An action-packed game, it stresses the need for good dribbling, tackling and shooting, as well as alertness, should there be the possibility of rebounds off the goalkeeper. (Sometimes the easiest goals in soccer are the result of goalkeepers who mis-handle or block the ball, giving the attentive player a golden opportunity.)

58

The winner is the first to score three goals. He then has the privilege of choosing whether to go in goal or stay "out". If he stays out, he chooses the player who goes "in". The existing goalkeeper cannot stay in for a second spell unless by full agreement of all players.

Summary

Remember that ideal practice conditions will not always be readily available. Suitable rebound walls exist, but may need some searching out. The illustrations in Practices 2 and 3 show authentic goals and a real soccer field. These may not be on hand, so improvise your own practice area.

𝄞𝄞 SECTION II

Shooting is fundamental to soccer, for without shots and goals, the game becomes meaningless. It is in this situation that the coach – Mum and Dad or whoever – can really inspire and motivate young players. A little stimulation and enthusiasm from adults will guarantee great fun, plenty of action, thrilling practice and much satisfaction for both player and coach.

In the Skills Chapters, 1 to 12, I have attempted to present as many of the practices as possible in game form, or at least in a competitive situation. In shooting practice the game requirement is not as necessary, since the objective is obvious, and the reward of scoring a goal is satisfaction and achievement in itself. Nevertheless, targets and challenges will be given.

Practice 4

In this practice, any number from two to five can be actively involved. First, an area is set up with a goal (*illustration 59*). The coach acts as the "server" to start the practice. He is positioned centrally, approximately five to 10 yards outside the penalty area. Two to three yards inside the penalty box is one attacking player marked by a defender. Disregarding for the moment the other two players outside the penalty area and the goalkeeper, here is how the practice works:

The coach passes the ball to the attacker who must try, with his back to goal, to "get turned" for an opportunity to shoot for goal. The defender's task is to try to ensure that the attack is unsuccessful. This he can best do by preventing the attacker from turning or by tackling him as he

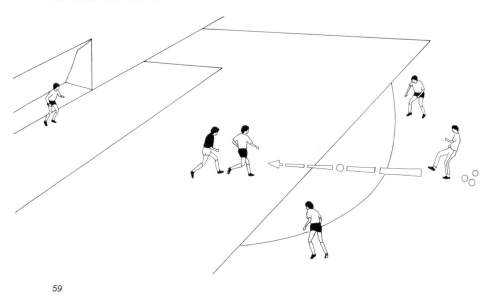

59

turns. If the attacking player finds he cannot turn past the defender, he should then play the ball back to the coach to start again.

When more players are available, use a goalkeeper and then consider the positions of the players outside the penalty area. They are restricted in that they are not allowed to enter the penalty area. So if the player in the penalty area chooses to lay the ball back, the players outside must shoot for goal – first time! The coach should rotate all players fairly frequently. One suggestion is to allow each player 10 shots; the competition would then be to see how many goals can be scored in each set of 10. The coach must encourage the attacker inside the penalty area to gamble on turning and shooting whenever possible. In the competition, therefore, it would be better to award four points for a goal scored on the turn by the scorer; for a goal scored from outside the penalty area, one point each for all three shooting players, with each player accumulating his own running totals throughout the complete sequence.

In this practice, encourage the attacker in the penalty area to push back the defender towards his own goal. This can be achieved by "walking away" the defender as far as he will go back (see Chapter 12, The Creation of Space). Such action will give the space to "come off the defender", to receive the ball and turn. Remember, there should be no infringements – if there are, award a penalty against a defender, or "no goal" if it is an offence by the attacking player.

Practice 5

Any number of players from one to 12 can undertake this practice. Ideally there should be one ball per person. As *illustration 60* shows, players stand seven to 10 yards outside the penalty area, and play a sharp ball into the arms of the coach. The coach sets up the type of ball to be shot at goal as the player moves into the penalty area. The advantage of the coach using his hands is that it is easier to provide a varied type of service which the player must accept in order to get his shot on goal. The coach may also act as a token defender to make the shooter aware of the need to avoid opposition.

In his service the coach can:

1. Roll the ball to one side for a shot
2. Throw it in the air for a volley
3. Bounce it on the ground for a half-volley
4. Lob it back towards the shooter as he comes forward so that he has to control it on his chest, and then get a shot in
5. Roll it towards the goal to simulate a through ball.

It is the task of the coach to relate the service to similar situations in the game, as suggested above, so that the practice becomes meaningful and challenging.

Again, numbers do not create a problem. Even if you have more than six you can always split youngsters into two groups, and play one against the other – but that is for Section III. In the case of three players, set up a competition where each player has a turn at goalkeeping and

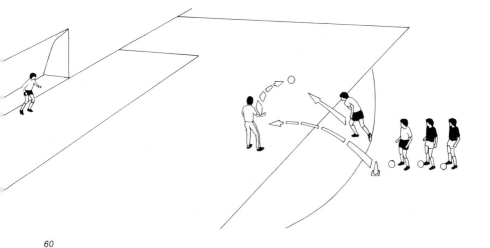

60

everyone has 20 shots at goal, the winner being the person with the highest goals total. With greater numbers, work in teams of two or three players per team.

Practice 6

In this practice the coach serves the ball by foot (preferably), or by hand. The ball is played across the front of the goal into the player coming from the marker cone just inside the penalty area (see *illustration 61*). This is a simple practice but a crucial one, as many scoring

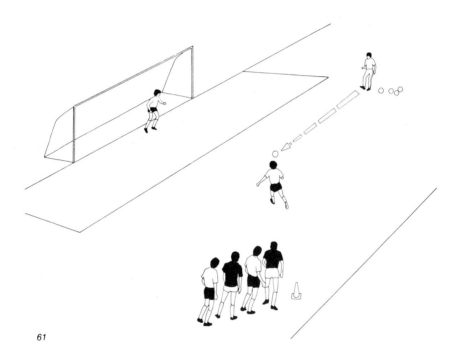

61

chances arise from this type of situation. To aid the practice, the goalkeeper must start on his line and can only move when the coach serves the ball, at which stage he can do whatever he thinks is possible to prevent the goal. It is important that after serving from one side, the service then comes from the opposite side of the penalty area so that players become skilled in finishing with both feet. Here again, it can be made competitive by playing individuals against one another, or with two small teams, one of which becomes the resting group that makes sure balls are retrieved and the server/coach supplied. The resting team nominates its own goalkeeper to oppose the shooters.

SECTION III

Most of the suggestions in Sections I and II can be adapted for use in the team practices. The problem is only one of organisation because of the greater numbers involved. You can split the team squad into two groups and make it competitive, with one group playing against the other. On the other hand, with an assistant coach, you can have one group working at one end of the field, with the second group at the other. The advantage of having one group acting as the fielders returning the balls quickly is that it will help keep the practice flowing. This in itself will increase player interest and heighten the competitive aspect of the sessions. An important consideration for the coach is that of service – unless it is fairly consistent, the players will complain that the coach is favouring one team. Consistent service, however, is not always possible or desirable. The winning group is the one scoring the most goals.

You will want to have an enthusiastic and capable goalkeeper in each group. When the group is taking its turn fielding, the nominated goalkeeper will be at the ready, trying the prevent the opposition from scoring – urged on by his team mates, of course, who will be cheering his every save.

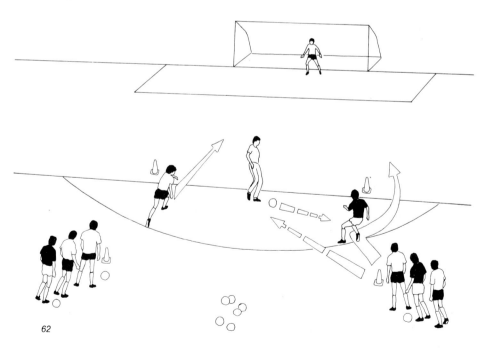

62

Practice 7

In this pairs shooting practice (see *illustration 62*), four cones are positioned with two groups of the same or similar numbers in line behind the cones, outside the penalty area. The two leading players in each group work as a pair. One of the two at the head of the line – it doesn't matter which one – has a ball. Indeed, there is a distinct advantage in making sure the first pass doesn't consistently come from one side. The ball is played in sharply and accurately to the coach positioned near the penalty spot. The coach sets up the pass by foot to the player on the left or the right – the choice is the coach's. The person receiving the pass for the shot at goal must go around the outside of the cone in the penalty area – either with the ball, if he has received it before reaching the cone, or without it, if the ball has been played by the coach at an angle behind the cone. In each case the player must go around the outside. The object of the practice is to produce an angled shot at goal.

While all this is happening, the player not receiving the ball moves into the penalty area using any type of run he chooses. As the non-receiver of the ball, he doesn't have to go outside the cone. His aim is to move in on goal to time his arrival just after the shot has reached the goalkeeper in anticipation of a mistake, and so pick up a rebound and score. His timing is critical. If he arrives too early, he will be unable to compose himself for the rebound shot; if he arrives too late, the goalkeeper – even having made a mistake – could recover.

This is a very real piece of the jigsaw of soccer, as many goals are scored from rebounds. In fact, "picking up the pieces" is a common soccer expression for this type of opportunist scoring. A popular and successful player in England was nicknamed "Sniffer" because of the way he sniffed out the half-chances in such situations. This exercise also gives players fine practice in shooting from an angle, where it is imperative to keep the ball low to cause the goalkeeper maximum difficulty. With a large squad, the coach can work with two groups – one shooting, one fielding – using the competition method.

Practice 8

This practice employs three groups of players and one or several goalkeepers (see *illustration 63*). Cones or suitable markers are placed on the edge of the penalty area to keep the group in line. The coach positions himself on the goal line a yard or two from the opposite goalpost to the file of defending players.

63

The sequence goes this way: the coach throws the ball out towards the first player in group A. His service simulates a headed clearance or a goalkeeper's mis-punch or a defender's half-clearance. The player from A moves onto the ball with the intention of shooting for goal.

However, at the very time the coach serves the ball, the front defender from file C is able to move out as quickly as he likes, to pressurise the attacker or block the shot. The player from file B is the supporting attacking player, looking for rebounds or possibly a pass – the pass is not generally recommended, as the opportunity to score depends on taking the advantage quickly or it will be too late.

This practice is an excellent test of the shooter's judgement, as how he decides to strike for goal must depend on the type of ball received, the oncoming defender, and the positon of the goalkeeper.

As the illustration indicates, organisation in terms of numbers is not difficult, and all of the large squad of players can be easily accommodated in one practice. After each strike at goal, the following sequence takes place: the player from file C goes to the back of file A; the player from file A, to the back of file B; the player from file B, to the back of file C; and so on.

Practice 9

Here is a shooting practice with very active opposition (see *illustration 64*). Basically, it is a two versus two in the penalty area. The coach, with a supply of balls, stands outside the "D" and plays the ball into either of the two attackers who are looking to get strikes at goal, either by turning and shooting themselves or by "laying off" the ball to the team mate in the penalty box for him to get a shot at goal. If neither of these situations produces the shooting opportunity, they then have a further alternative: they can play the ball back to either of the two players positioned outside the penalty area who must shoot first time, but who are not allowed to enter the penalty area themselves. Playing the ball back to the players outside the area should be the option least encouraged by the coach, and this can be reflected in awarding points (or praise) weighted in favour of the shot, or goal, created from the "in penalty area effort" as opposed to the easier alternative of playing the ball back to the players outside.

You can see from the illustration using eight players – four attackers, two defenders, plus two resting defenders – that a competitive situation can be set up whereby points are given for goals scored from 20 attempts at goal, with a weighting of four points for a goal from inside the penalty area and one point for a goal from the unmarked attackers outside the area. After 10 attempts, players are switched with the attacker inside the penalty area changing with those outside, and the two active defenders changing with the resting defenders. This is followed by the attackers then reversing roles with the defenders.

64

Nine players – or 10 with two goalkeepers – can be comfortably put to practise. Even a third group of players – four plus a goalkeeper – could be involved, although initially they would stand out of the practice, acting as fielders and awaiting their turn.

Another way to accommodate the full squad of 20 or more in shooting practices such as this one is by splitting the group into three teams, having two teams play a small-sided game (seven or eight a side) while the third is involved in the shooting practice. The teams are changed every 10 minutes or so. This is just another example of the coach using the numbers game to achieve the objective of the practice session.

Because it is impossible to know the exact numbers that will turn out for practice prior to a session and because of possible illness and injury, enjoyable time-gaining practices such as the circle game (Chapter 1, Practice 9) are strongly recommended. It's no different than going to the circus. Between the main acts, the clowns fill in and keep the interest bubbling while re-organisation takes place.

Practice 10
Shooting soccer

This practice is a modified version of change-soccer (Chapter 1, Practice 13) that has been adapted to encourage shooting (see *illustration 65*). In this case, a very short and relatively narrow field has been marked out by extending the penalty area by a further 10 yards or so. The illustration shows authentic goals at either end – which is ideal. It is unlikely, however, that you will have the luxury of portable, full-sized goals, so use corner flags. Better still, use one authentic goal of a soccer field, and improvise the second goal using corner flags. Change ends frequently to give equal time shooting at the real goal.

The small size of the field and the proximity of the goals, no matter where the ball is within the field, should encourage every player to think goal and so shoot on every possible occasion. In order to make the practice realistic, the goalkeepers are not allowed to shoot. If the coach has a good supply of balls, he can position himself on the sidelines and throw another ball in when shots go over the bar, past the post, or out of the field of play, and so maintain momentum and alertness. The "change" rule as applied in Chapter 1, Practice 13, can be used, but the players should find this activity so intense that it shouldn't be necessary. Players will welcome a rest and can be changed over in a more leisurely manner. Both groups of one team compete against the combined players of the other as far as the score line is concerned. One further advantage of not using the change-soccer rule is that the off-

65

the-field players can act as fielders, and so help keep the momentum going on the field without being concerned about making a fast changeover.

Numbers can be adjusted in the practice depending on players present, so a two versus two, three versus three, even a four versus four is an acceptable situation. Thus with the goalkeepers (four can be used), combinations of players from 10 to 20 are easily accommodated.

Conclusion

You will have no problem convincing players that shooting is a valuable skill requiring considerable practice. Nor will motivation be lacking. Therefore the coach has no excuse to avoid this vital aspect of the game! He can win friends and respect by putting on realistic practices such as those referred to in this chapter, and also give his players a much better chance of winning matches through regular shooting sessions. Winning shouldn't be the all-important consideration in the coaching of young players, but it does help!

Chapter 4
CROSSING FROM THE WINGS

〄 SECTION I

Crossing the ball is one of the most essential skills in soccer. It is also probably the most difficult to master. Therefore, regular practice in crossing is a must.

Teams, whether they use orthodox wingers or not, must ensure that they have players running into flank positions to use the full width of the field and so open up the defence. Let's begin by looking at some of the special considerations that have to be overcome:

1. Normally the player on the wing is moving with the ball at speed inside the touch line and towards the goal line.
2. He is required to cross the ball at something close to a right angle (90 degrees) from his direction of run.
3. Often he is under challenge from an opponent.
4. His cross must be hit firmly and *accurately*.

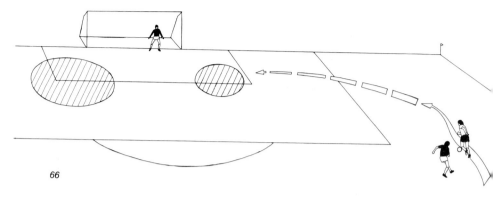

66

The accuracy referred to above is represented in *illustration 66* by the two shaded areas close to the goal – the "near post" and the "far post" areas – and most crosses should be aimed for one or the other. The near and far post areas are so critical because they are the most difficult areas to defend, both for the goalkeeper and his fellow defenders.

Near post

A slight touch of a near post cross from an attacker – even a defender – might be enough to score. The goalkeeper is compelled to remain near his goal line until a cross is on its way, whether it's near or far. He has no other choice. He cannot afford to anticipate a cross. Therefore, the goalkeeper has limited time to move to the near post ball. When he does, it will often result in his having to stretch to get to the ball both over and past players of both teams who have gathered around the near post space. This will put him under considerable pressure, with mis-judgement and mis-handling constant risks.

Far post

The far post cross normally forces defenders and the goalkeeper to recover backwards to either head or catch the ball. A well-stationed attacking player, on the other hand, moving onto the ball from a deep position on the edge of the penalty area, has the distinct advantage of moving forwards and towards the ball. The attacker can see everything and should be able to leap higher from his more favourable run.

Anyone moving into a flank attacking position must take all the factors mentioned into account in order to make a successful cross.

Here are some tips:

1. When time – and the opposition – allow, a player should change the angle of his run slightly to make the approach to striking the ball more favourable (see *illustration 67*).

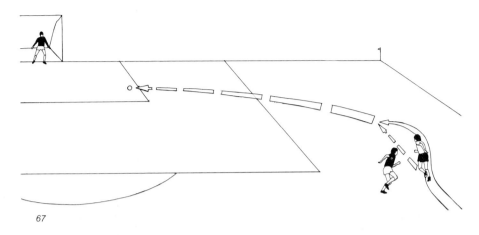

67

68

69

70   71

2. At the same time, if the forward movement to the ball can be controlled and steadied just before the cross, then a final split second of composure can be won for setting up the striking of the ball.

3. If a marking opponent is very near, then a "fake", or a touch of the ball to one side of the opponent, or both, will probably be necessary to open up enough space to cross the ball around the opponent (see *illustrations 68, 69 and 70, 71*). You'll notice from the *illustration 70* that it is not even necessary to gain one or two yards on your opponent. Six to 12 inches may be all that is needed to open up enough space to bend the cross round the defending player and into the scoring zone.

4. Whether points 1, 2 and 3 are at work or not, the striking foot must be "wrapped around" the outside of the ball (see *illustration 71*) to compensate for the forward momentum, and to avoid slicing the ball over the bar or the goal line. How much the foot wraps around the ball will depend on the speed of the ball, the momentum of the player and how much bend is desired on the cross.

5. Should it be near or the far post? That depends on the circumstances. Wherever possible, the crossing player should look up just prior to crossing (and at any other time he can in the lead-up to the cross) in order to assess which would be the best cross – near or far. Sometimes it is not possible to evaluate the situation accurately, par-

72

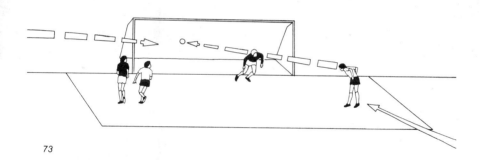

73

ticularly when being challenged, but that needn't prevent the cross from still going in – guessing near or far, never in between. If the fellow attackers of the player crossing the ball are moving forward to support the impending cross, they should be making runs into both the near and far post spaces anyway.

Let's now discuss the basic differences, other than the distances involved, between near and far post crosses:

The near post cross should be arriving in the near post space at head height or lower, to enable the ball to be diverted into goal or to be deflected. It should also be hit with reasonable pace both to aid the effectiveness of the header or deflection and to catch defenders by surprise (*illustration 72*). (Refer also to Chapter 5, Heading.)

Note: "Head height" is the most effective at the near post because it is the easiest ball to divert or deflect. Timing a deflection or striking a shot at goal with the foot requires real skill – with little margin for error.

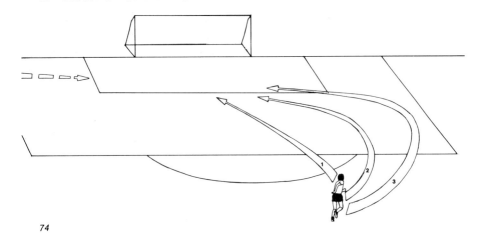

74

The far post cross *must* clear all players positioned around the near post and the central area – otherwise it fails to become a far post cross (see *illustration 73*). At the same time, it should not be so high that it comes down "with snow on it". A very high ball is too long in the air and gives the goalkeeper and defenders time to reposition. It will also not have enough "pace" on it to allow the attacker to convert the cross into a powerful goal-scoring attempt. So it should be *just clear* of the players and the outstretched hands of the goalkeeper – positioned in the near and middle part of the area – and arrive at the far post where a good leap would enable the ball to be met with the head (*illustration 73*).

Practices for crossing are slightly more difficult to organise than most other skills practices, and it is not always possible for them to be presented in game form. Sometimes a more formal practice situation is necessary. The temptation may well be to leave it until next time, and the next time, but I would implore you not to do that. The skill of crossing is so important that it *must* be practised, even If It means a little inconvenience.

Note – Before looking at the practices: In consulting the illustrations that appear in Sections I, II and III, you will notice that with nearly all the attacking runs to meet crossed balls, the first part of the run is *away* from the man with the ball (see *illustration 74*). This is deliberate.

Moving away from the ball gives the attacker the opportunity to get on the "blind side" of the defenders (see Chapter 12, The Creation of Space). It also improves the angle of the final run to attack the cross. The objective should be the same as that of ball control (see Chapter 8), where moving into the line of flight of the ball is critical.

Time is the key factor, however, in the runs to attack crosses. There just may not be enough time to move away before moving in for the cross, so run 1 has to be used – and it is very unlikely there will be the time to get perfectly into the line of flight, indicated in run 3. Run 2 shows the middle run, which is normally the most effective one to attack the cross, and get above and in front of defenders in the time available to an attacking player.

Notice, too, that in most diagrams the cross is shown reaching the near and far post area on the edge of the six-yard box. As long as a cross is not "floated" in too high, six to seven yards is just a little too far for the goalkeeper to feel confident about coming for the ball. The six-yard line gives the crosser a guide to aim for.

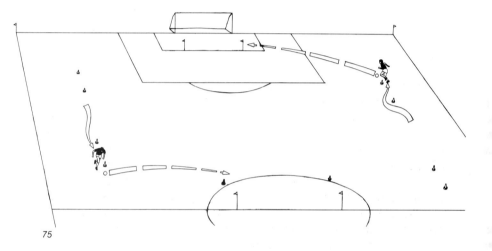

75

Practice 1

This practice is for a player on his own. A fairly large space is needed, preferably half the size of a soccer field. It is useful, but not essential, to have soccer field markings. What *is* essential, however, is to be willing to run a long way! As you can see from *illustration 75*, a number of markers have been set out. The wing markers (cones, stones, posts – anything) are there to be beaten – imaginary opponents – and then the ball is crossed, using the markers at the near and far post zones as indicators to help assess the quality of the cross. The player has to jog across the field to retrieve the ball and then continue – circular fashion – on the other side, using an improvised goal on the half-way line.

A youngster should award himself marks out of 10 for each cross, and must decide in his own mind whether it is to be a near or far post cross. If a proper soccer field is not available, improvise all the goals and touch lines, and the near and far post zones, with your own posts and markings. Remember to reverse the direction of the practice so you are crossing with the left foot, too. A practice such as this one, on your own is physically hard work, but keep on jogging!

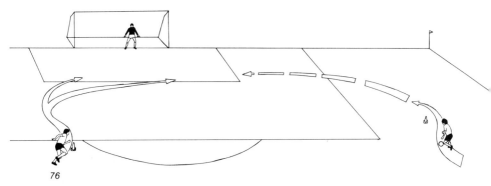

76

Practice 2

Here is a practice for two or three players. *Illustration 76* shows the crossing player starting from a deep position, attacking and going past a marker to cross for the second player, who attacks the ball in an attempt to score. The winger can vary his run by using his imagination. He can fake, take the ball to the goal line before crossing, check and pull the ball back onto his left foot – or his right if he is on the other side of the field, and so on. The two players should develop an understanding – by use of signals, by talking and by visual assessment – to decide whether to attack the near or the far post. Obviously, it is not ideal to have played a great cross into the far post area if the player attacking the cross has made a run into the near post, so this is a first-class practice to help you "get your act together".

With three players available, use a goalkeeper. Make sure that all players return to the original starting positions after each cross – particularly the "starter post" just outside the penalty box. This is very important as the player attacking the ball should not be standing waiting for the cross when it comes in. Don't forget to repeat the same practice from the left side, and also to change around starting positions frequently – say, every 10 crosses.

Practice 3

This is a practice for three or four players (if four are available, use a goalkeeper), although larger numbers can easily be accommodated.

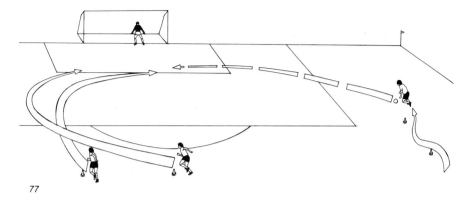

77

Refer to *illustration 77*. The organisation here is almost identical to that of Practice 2, except there are two players, to attack the cross. This allows the crossing player to choose who to cross to – the one at the near post or the second player at the far post. The runs of the two attackers are critical, and I recommend you read the section on attacking heading (Chapter 5, page 92).

Make sure all players return to the starting positions before recommencing the practice, and have everyone change around every so often (10 crosses each). When every player has had his turn in every position, start again with crosses from the opposite side. As most players are naturally right-footed, it is easy to neglect crosses from the left. Don't be too concerned should the quality not be as good on the less comfortable side. Players who prefer kicking with the right foot must practise crossing from the left side and vice versa. A pleasant surprise may await you if you really wrap your foot around the ball when crossing with your less comfortable foot. It's not as difficult as you may think.

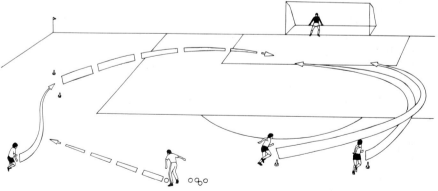

78

Keep practising your crossing techniques – the benefits are many. Heading and shooting for goal, spectacular goalkeeping saves, great crosses and diving headers are among the most exciting parts of the game.

⚽ ⚽ SECTION II

When a group of young friends get together with a soccer ball, the coach or the parent comes into his own. In Section I, I have encouraged young players to practise crossing by themselves, and so they should. But an adult can be of tremendous help, and is able to control the practice more realistically.

It is vitally important, for instance, that after each cross and shot youngsters return to their original starting positions. Otherwise, you can very quickly end up with attacking players waiting at the near and far post zones for the cross to arrive. The situation rarely happens in the game – most times, the attackers will be offside, for one thing. Attacking players, in the main, will be moving forward and out of the midfield area at the same time as a flank player moves down the wing. While they do so, the opposing central defenders will be on the move, retreating into the scoring zone, ready to defend against the cross.

Practice 4

This practice is identical to Practices 2 and 3 of Section I, except that here, the coach controls its organisation (see *illustration 78*). He can act as the server and start the practice by playing a pass to the crosser. This is a more realistic situation. The service can be varied so that the wing player receives the ball either at his feet or played forward into space to move onto. The "space" ball brings another dimension to the practice as the wing player now has a decision to make – should he strike the cross first time, or take the ball on, move further down the flanks, and then cross? The coach will have to adjust numbers according to how many players there are, and the positions he wants them to assume.

Practice 5

This is a progression of Practice 4, and will depend on the numbers available. The crossing player is now confronted by a defender

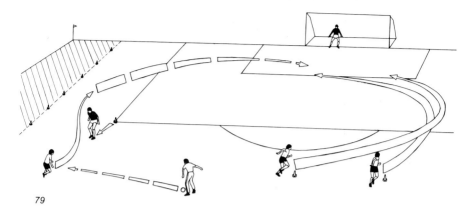

79

(*illustration 79*) who, in the early stages, could well be the coach. He can act like a token defender to make the crossing player aware of an opponent without actually trying to win the ball in a tackle. The illustration shows six people involved in the practice but the coach will organise the session as numbers dictate. For instance, it is not essential to have a goalkeeper all the time, and it will depend on whether you can designate both a server and a defender. If there are insufficient numbers for a server, the crosser himself can start the practice by simply running the ball at defenders. Better still, one of the central attackers can play the ball out wide to the player on the wing, and then turn to move into the penalty area to attack the anticipated cross.

To motivate the players, award marks out of 10 for the cross and the shot at goal, and the goalkeeper's efforts to save. Remember that young players may not be strong enough in their kicking to reach the far post from the wide positions of a normal soccer pitch. For them, narrow the field by putting in place another touch line, using cones or markers.

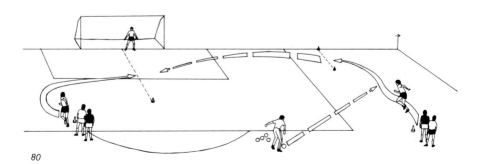

80

 **SECTION III**

In the team practice, the coach needs to be very aware of his young players' abilities. For instance, six- to nine-year-olds will have great difficulty making any sense of crossing the ball if they cannot yet kick strongly enough even to reach the goal. That does not mean omitting crossing. What it *does* mean, however, is that the coach must narrow down the touch lines to meet his young players' level of abilities (see *illustration 79*). This will enable them to see the value of good crossing as well as understand where are the best areas to aim the crosses.

Practice 6
Crossing and heading competition

In this session, the team squad can be divided into two teams, preferably with a recognised goalkeeper in each. *Illustration 80* shows one team split evenly in two, one half at a cone inside the penalty area, the other half at the flank cone. The other team takes up position behind the goal and retrieves the balls. The position of the flank cones can be adjusted according to players' age and ability. The penalty area is split into halves by markers (bibs, or lines) – the front half for near post crosses, and the back half for far post crosses. The cone nearest the penalty spot is the starting position for the near post crosses, the other cone for the far post crosses.

Here is how the practice functions:
1. The coach, with a supply of balls, serves into the leading flank cone player.
2. The crossing player must go past and outside the cone; he cannot come inside the imaginary line between the cone on the field and the one on the goal line to cross the ball.
3. Goals can only be scored by the head.
4. When the rule is near post crosses, the attacking header *must* take place in the front part as indicated by the marking line from the centre of the goal to the penalty spot. Here a marker is obviously necessary. Conversely, far post crosses can be scored only from the back half of the penalty area.
5. The goalkeeper must start each time on the goal line.
6. The sequence is: after a player crosses, he joins the heading file, and after heading, joins the crossing file.
7. The goalkeeper is from the off-field group.
8. The coach decides how many crosses per group (it may be 20 or 30),

after which the non-active group comes on and the others go off. The coach keeps score, and the group scoring the most goals wins.

9. The full sequence of the total practice is:
   a. Near post crosses from the right – both groups
   b. Near post crosses from the left – both groups
   c. Far post crosses from the right – both groups
   d. Far post crosses from the left – both groups.

A running total is kept by the coach or "sets" are played. The coach has to be on his toes to keep track of the score and how many crosses have taken place, as well as eliminate any cheating and skulduggery.

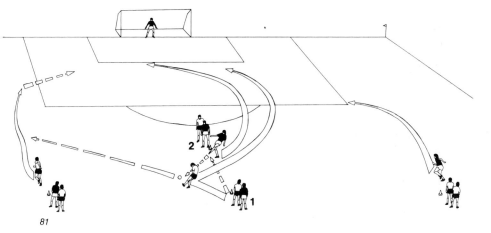

81

Practice 7

Now players work in four groups at each marker cone (see *illustration 81;* note in the file at the central cone nearest the goal, that the players are standing with their back to goal).

The practice sequence is:

1. The leading player at the half-way line starts the practice by playing a ball into the colleague at the other central zone (2) who is standing with his back to goal. Player 2 returns the ball to 1 (setting-up pass), and 1 first times the ball to one of the wing players – right or left. The pass can be played either into the feet of the flank player or into space for the wing player to run onto.

2. The winger works the ball down the wing, while at the same time players 1 and 2 are moving quickly toward and into the penalty area to attack the impending cross. The winger on the opposite flank to the pass moves in to support the attack. Most often, he will take a position around the angle of the penalty area (see illustration), and he is restricted to one-touch only – preferably a shot, should he receive the ball from a cross that has overrun the two central attackers.

3. 1 & 2 also have one touch of the ball each – *maximum* – although it doesn't necessarily have to be a shot. It may be to set up a shot from a partner. The one-touch rule helps in simulating game conditions, where time in the penalty area is nearly always scarce.

4. The goalkeeper can take up whatever position he believes is best to defend the goal.

5. The rule is alternate sides for each cross from each group. So, having played out to the left once, next time it must be to the right.

6. The practice operates with successive waves of four attackers from each of the four files, but not until the field has been cleared of the previous wave. Each group of four keeps a tally of its successful attacks, and players change their starting positions regularly.

The practice can be progressed by introducing one defender who remains in the penalty area, but first make certain the players are ready for opposed heading situations (consult Chapter 5). Alternatively, the coach can put himself in the penalty area to become a token defender, thus using his own discretion to avoid possible injuries.

The leading group is identified on a regular basis, and a winner declared at the end of the practice. With very young players, be prepared to reduce the distances involved in the starting positions, otherwise it could be too difficult for them.

Practice 8

This practice emphasises crossing, and players attacking crosses to get strikes at goal (see *illustration 82*). The area has to be carefully

82

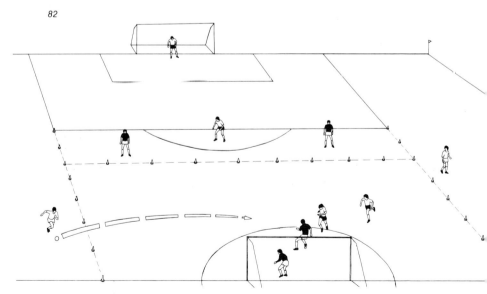

marked out, and ideally half an authentic soccer field can be used. The field is then subdivided by means of markers, a half-way line is put in, and a wing corridor is placed on either side. Each player is restricted to a particular area:

1. The attacking and defending players must stay in that half of the field where they are originally placed. They cannot go into the wing corridor.
2. The wingers must stay in their respective corridors.
3. The practice sequences run as follows:
   a. The goalkeeper starts by throwing the ball to one of the wingers.
   b. The winger moves down the flank and crosses near or far post for the two attacking players.
   c. The defender, along with the goalkeeper, works to repel the attack.
   d. The wingers have no allegiance – they attack and cross the ball in the direction of the player from whom they receive it.
   e. Goals can be scored only as a direct result of a crossed ball, including a set-up ball and first-time shot. Therefore, if a cross fails, the ball can be played out again by an attacker to one of the wingers for another cross, and that is the only way an attack on goal can be sustained.
   f. Even though restricted to one half of the field, defenders can pass to their attacking team mates. Goals, however, can be scored only as a direct result of a cross from the wing.
   g. Goalkeepers, whenever they receive the ball, *must* throw to a winger.

While this practice has been illustrated with 10 players working, and an effective two versus one in each half, a coach can feel free to modify the practice in terms of numbers. For example, try three versus two, rather than two versus one, and so involve 14 players. Or perhaps use four wingers, with the left and right winger for each side and a limitation of each winger to the attacking half of the flank corridor (see the line in *illustration 82*) – a good test for the throwing accuracy of the goal-keeper.

Practice 8, although promising an excellent work-out, is admittedly more complex than the others so if you are a little unsure, don't worry!

Practices 6 and 7 are simpler but first rate, and those in Section I and II can easily be adapted to the team practice. So get cracking on crossing and as the old pros used to say, "See you at the far post".

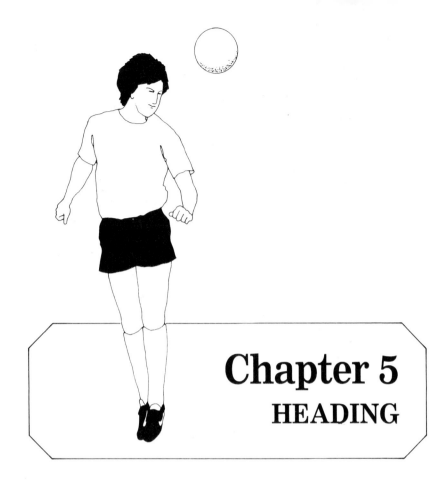

Chapter 5
HEADING

𝄋 SECTION I

Heading is without a doubt the most difficult skill to coach and to learn in the game. The technique of heading a ball in isolation – without any opposition involved – is difficult enough, but when one player is challenging against others, it can become hazardous. The fact is, almost all other techniques involved in soccer are *natural*. Kicking and controlling the ball, dribbling past opponents, goalkeepers diving to catch a ball, even players tackling one another to gain possession – all these actions would happen automatically, if a group of first-time players were thrown together and quickly told the fundamentals of the game. Choosing to be struck on the head, however, is not natural. But it can be a most spectacular and effective skill.

Let's begin by considering the mechanics of actually striking the ball with the head.

Illustration 83 clearly shows the part of the head that should strike the ball. If the ball is any lower on the forehead, the result will bring tears to

83

your eyes, or at least a sore nose. Any higher, and you'll be rewarded with a sore head, as the top of the skull is relatively thin. The forehead is the flattest part of the head with the thickest bone coverage, thereby giving protection to the brain. As well, the eyes can watch the ball almost right onto the forehead.

To make sure you are using the right part of the head and the right technique, try the following practices.

Practice 1

Working on your own, or with friends, find a solid, flat rebound surface such as a brick or concrete wall. Stand approximately two to three yards back from the wall, throw the ball up and attempt to keep it rebounding against the wall (see *illustration 84*).

To achieve any success, it will be necessary for the player to use the correct forehead method to maintain the sequence. He will also need to watch the ball right onto the forehead. Should a player close his eyes, the instinctive reaction is to duck – usually resulting in the ball hitting the top of the head. Apart from a poor, uncontrolled header, it's painful! (*Illustration 85*.)

A regular soccer ball may prove "hard" going for steady practice of this repetitive exercise, so the use of a tennis ball is recommended. There will be less discomfort, a tennis ball is inexpensive, and it is very

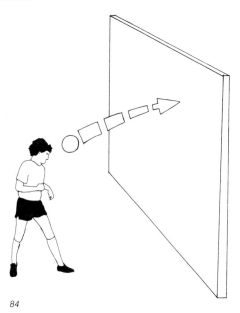

84

85

WRONG

challenging. Once you're accustomed to practising with the tennis ball, begin setting targets. At first, five continuous headers. Then 10, 20, 40 – even 100.

Practice 2

Using a regular soccer ball, the idea is to keep the ball up using the head only – no rebound wall here. A youngster practising in this way can end up with a slightly stiff neck, but if he has been successful in keeping the sequence going, then the correct part of the head must have been used (see *illustration 86*).

Once a player becomes comfortable with Practices 1 and 2, heading can be progressed to bring some power to the heading action – in order to propel the ball for distance or into the back of the net. The power for heading comes from the whole of the body. The power-producing body

86

87   88

action (see *illustrations 87 and 88*) is transmitted into the ball obviously – but only finally – from the head. You can develop a feel for the power-producing action by rocking backwards and forwards from a sideways position without a ball. Just do it. You will get the idea.

Most headers are preceded by a run, followed by a leap (see *illustrations 89, 90 and 91*). The run and jump give the extra power and the height to project the ball on its way.

An extra, final thrust can be achieved by snapping the body forward at the moment of impact – without ducking the head. However, use the snapping action with care, as much will depend on whether opposition is present. If this is the case, it will probably be necessary to remain upright to win the challenge. Anyway, the snap should never be exaggerated or body power will be lost. It's simply a little final thrust when circumstances permit.

Sometimes the ball may be dropping just where a player is positioned, so it becomes impossible to get a run at it. Even so, it is far better – if time allows – for the player to drop off a yard or so, to enable him to come forward to attack the ball and power it on its way. Or at the very least, if a step back is not possible, the rocking action mentioned earlier should be considered. This, as you will see later, gives the momentum necessary to challenge successfully as well as producing power.

Practice 3

As *Illustration 92* shows, one player stands behind the line and another, approximately five yards away (distance will vary according to players' age and size). The player with the ball lobs it to his partner who steps back, and then comes forward to power the header back to – or, if possible, over his partner. If he is successful, then the thrower retreats further back. To progress the practice, the ball can be thrown higher to enable the player heading to come forward and leap for the ball. Compete to see who can power head the ball furthest, using the line as the boundary beyond which the player making the header must not go, and marking the first bounce as the distance of each header.

89

90

91

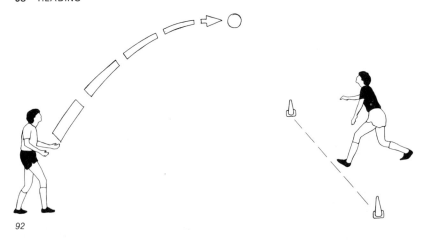

92

Because players are required, sooner or later, to head the ball in soccer, serious consideration should be given the next aspect of heading – that is, competing for the ball in the air **against opposition**. The younger the players, the less concern there should be with introducing the opposition factor. Youngsters, by and large, are sensible, and will not compete against an opponent in the air until they feel ready to do so – unless they are goaded by the coach, their own friends or overly enthu-

93

94   95

siastic parents on the touch line. So patience is the watchword for both the coach and young players.

The best way to approach opposed heading is *gradually, skilfully* and with correct *technique*. That confidence, knowledge of how to protect yourself from injury, can make all the difference. Study *illustrations 93, 94, and 95*. The players in *93* and *95* are in poor position. In the case of *93*, standing behind an opponent "square-on" can often result in the back of the opponent's head striking the nose, mouth or eyes of the back player, because the player's face is unprotected.

In *94*, the player demonstrates good position; he is protecting himself without limiting his ability to win the aerial challenge. In fact, just the opposite. By turning his shoulder into the opponent, he forms a battering ram with which to help the physical challenge. This is perfectly fair, and within the rules of the game, as long as the arms and elbows are not raised. What's more, the shoulder provides a shield, should the opponent attempt to back-head. The turned positions, however, should only be slight. If it's exaggerated, the opponent's challenge can spin the player out of a strong position and into a poor challenging one (see *illustration 95*).

Practice 4

Initially, ease into this type of opposed heading by using an opponent who offers only a token challenge. As you can see in *illustration 96*, the server with the ball is approximately seven to eight yards away, and lobs the ball over and above the front player for the back player to challenge and head back to or over the server. The front player acts more as a distraction at first, but then physically backs into the heading player without making a full challenge. This is an important exercise, allowing players to familiarise themselves with opposed heading. Frequent practice in this situation is invaluable so that the player feels completely at ease, both with heading the ball and with the presence of a challenging opponent. The intensity of this practice can be increased as players become more accomplished – but don't try to progress too quickly, and don't move on to Practice 5 until everyone seems ready.

Practice 5

This practice begins with a marked-out area (see *illustration 97*). The goal at the back of the rectangle containing the two players measures three to five feet high. Neither player is allowed in the final part of the rectangle. This practice can be presented in the form of a game. The serving player's objective is to try to chip the ball to score in the goal, for

96

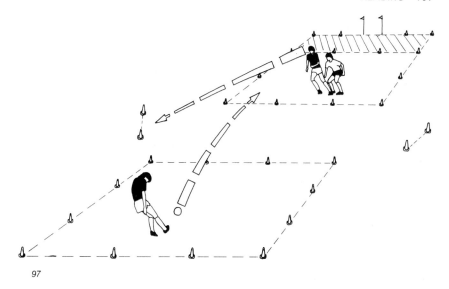

97

two points. However, he cannot kick a dead ball. He must touch the ball
and then kick it with the second touch. The ball must be judged to pass
under the bar to score, even if there is no bar. Alternatively, he can chip
the ball up for his team mate in the opposite square who can score in
two ways: he can back-head the ball so that it lands first bounce into the
circle for two points, or he can head it down to pass between the small
cone goals to the right and left of the rectangle. The ball must pass
through the goals at ground height – six inches or less – for one point.

The defender must do everything possible to stop the ball from going
behind him, without his leaving the square. If the ball bounces in the
shaded area, then the defender concedes a point to the other two. If the
defender wins the ball in the air and heads it back to bounce in the
server's square (or beyond), the defender receives three points. The
first to score six points is the winner, with the two attackers combining
their points versus the defender.

Heading in the game itself

Unfortunately you cannot progress practices in a game and organise
situations to graduate the degree of difficulty. Circumstances arise and
demand action. With heading – particularly at an early age – my advice
would be that if there is no one challenging, and you have worked on
your heading techniques as in Practices 1, 2, and 3, go to it. If it looks as
if you will have to challenge for a ball in the air in competition with
opponents, and you are unsure – hold back. **But don't turn away from**

the ball, don't close your eyes, and don't duck you head. Otherwise, you might be in for an unpleasant surprise. Watch the ball. Size up the situation. And then, when you feel confident and positive, take up a good position in relation to the challenging opponent and go for it.

Practice 6

Two players stand four to five yards apart (see *illustration 98*). The ball is thrown up first to start the heading. The purpose is to keep the sequence going. No player may head the ball twice consecutively – if that happens, the sequence is over. Keep track of your record, and then try to beat it. If there are four players, have a pairs competition. If there are three, take turns.

Eventually, work with three in a triangle – much more difficult as the direction of the incoming header has to be changed.

Practice 7

Here, a goal is set up (if you have a soccer field to work on, so much the better) and a crossed-ball service is played in from the right and later

98

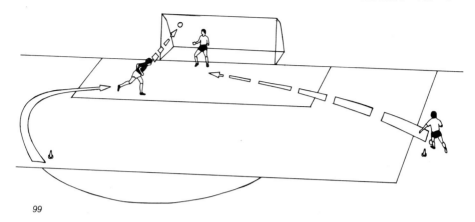

99

from the left for a player to attack in an attempt to head a goal. The heading player should move back to the marker cone after each cross so that he comes in to attack the ball as a forward would in a game (*illustration 99*). As the main purpose is to practise heading, it is very important that the service from the wings is the right one. Make sure the distance the crosser is serving from is not too demanding. If difficulty is experienced in crossing the ball, a thrown service can be used. Obviously it is more realistic if there is a good kicked cross but if that is not happening, at least throwing the ball will guarantee the heading practice. Take turns in moving from server to header – and to goalkeeper if there are three.

One tip: perhaps the most difficult header for a goalkeeper to deal with is one which is *down and away* from the keeper. Goalkeepers most times find a ball in the air easier to save. Without a bounce it is simpler to judge. So practise heading down powerfully to hit the goal line and thus bounce the ball into the back of the net.

Look at Practices 2 and 3 in Chapter 4 on Crossing, and adapt these to Practice 7. The practices involve crossing, heading and goalkeeping.

🏐🏐 SECTION II

Very often Dad or Mum will be asked to help youngsters learn heading. Parents are naturally concerned that their children practise this skill correctly and safely. With this in mind, it is recommended that the earlier parts of this chapter be read thoroughly and, if necessary, reread. Young players may need particular help in the setting up and the conducting of Practices 1, 2, 4, and 6.

Once they are ready for heading practice involving opposition, help can be given in the organisation of Practice 4. Leave Practice 5 until the young players are more accomplished. Often, the parent/coach can be the key factor in overcoming the fear of heading.

If you have access to a soccer field, pack your charges into the car for an opportunity to work on the practices in Chapter 4. Youngsters will really enjoy such a session and so will the coach. What's more, your presence and your organisational assistance will make it really live.

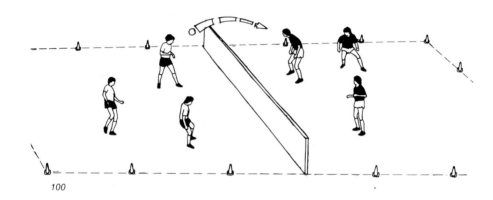

100

Practice 8
Head tennis

Head tennis is a game soccer players the world over enjoy. It is an improvised version of tennis that is easily set up anywhere there is a little space. Cones, ropes, sticks, stones, and chalk lines can again be used to mark out a rectangle and to put in a "net" to divide the "court" (see *illustration 100*). It's best to use a rope or divider for the net to encourage more heading, but if these are unavailable, you can designate a no-man's-land.

Rules

1. Any number up to six a side can be accommodated: one versus one, two versus two, uneven numbers such as five versus four, etc.
2. Service is from the back line of the court, over the net. The ball must bounce, in the opposite court.

3. Any part of the head or body can keep the ball up – except the hands and arms.

4. Once the ball has bounced after serving, it is not permitted to touch the ground again until it passes over the net.

5. Each group is allowed as many touches as is necessary or desired, either individually or collectively, before playing the ball across the net.

6. When the ball goes across the net, it must bounce inside the court or the point is lost, although the other team can elect to intercept the ball before it bounces.

7. The scoring rules should be agreed upon. It is suggested you play 10 or 20 up, and change the service every five points.

Apart from the obvious enjoyment factor, the game provides excellent practice in heading, ball manipulation and controlled volleying.

SECTION III

The team coach dealing with heading has a tremendous responsibility. He needs to be extremely careful and yet spend as much time as possible working on heading techniques and confidence practices, such as those outlined in the earlier part of the chapter. Because he needs to prepare players for competition, sooner or later he will have to deal with the realities of headed situations occurring in the games. Please reread and evaluate the remarks I have made on pages 97, 98 and 99 of this chapter.

To ignore the necessity of practising heading will only increase the fear of the technique. This may result in a greater number of injuries because of the lack of opportunity to learn, and the consequent inability

101

to deal with what is a potentially dangerous situation. But presented in an intelligent and responsible way, heading can leave young players with the wonderful sense of achievement that comes from having mastered a difficult technique, as they become skilled in the aerial game.

All the practices covered in this chapter are readily adapted to the team practice. Practice 6, for example, can be developed by splitting the team into pairs. The whole squad can then benefit from useful practice in an enjoyable and challenging situation. Which pair can keep the sequence going for more than five headers? More than 10? More than 12?

Practice 9

This practice is a team adaptation of Practice 6. After each header, the player turns and goes to the back of the file or, to make it more active, he can move across to join the back of the opposite file (see *illustration 101*). Two teams of eight to 10 can compete against one another. The coach must ensure that the rule "one headed touch only" is adhered to, and that players don't go out of turn to preserve the sequence, following a misplaced header.

Practice 10

Practice 5 will benefit both defensive and creative heading. If you look at *illustration 97*, the player receiving the chipped service is getting first-class practice in the requirement of midfield heading, although it appears to be set up like a defender versus attacker situation. Practice 5 can be progressed into a more meaningful exercise for the team, and at the same time involve more players.

Practice 11

In *illustration 102* the server – this can be the coach – begins by serving a high ball into the penalty area. The defender, if he can, must challenge and clear the ball away from the penalty area. Of course he must not foul (a penalty), nor will he be able to win the ball every time. If he tries to do so, he will put himself at a disadvantage in certain situations, for instance, when the ball is dropping short. The attacker in the penalty area challenges the defender for every ball and tries to play back, at an angle, a header for one of the two supporting attackers outside the penalty area to shoot. They are limited to one-touch only so it needs to be a first time shot. The defender continues to react to the situation

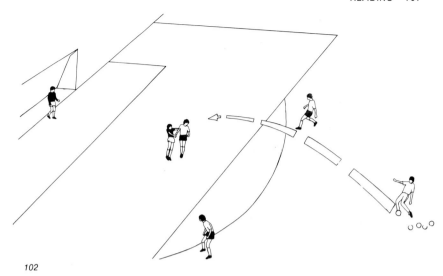

102

until the attack is concluded, and therefore does whatever he thinks best to prevent a goal. For example, if he does not win the aerial challenge and the ball is headed back to the two players outside the area, he can move across and try to block the shot. Be careful, though, that the defender does not anticipate too soon by moving across to block the shot. Allow his opponent to fake a header and spin in behind the defender if he is anticipating too much.

If the team coach has a large squad, he can organise another group working in the same way at the other end of the field. Alternatively, depending on space and numbers, he can make it two versus two in the penalty area, with two or three attackers outside the penalty area.

To make it a competitive situation, the coach can pit the goalkeeper and defender against the rest – 10 unsuccessful attempts at goal count as one goal for the defenders; every authentic goal counts as one for the attackers. The coach must take care to condition the practice so that it begins with a high ball into the penalty area. This can be achieved by disallowing scoring from a low service. Otherwise the realism of the practice is lost.

Different headers

It is of paramount importance that players acquire the following skills:

1. The correct technique of heading.
2. The ability to protect their bodies, particularly their faces and heads, when making an aerial challenge.

3. The confidence to head the ball without consciously thinking about the incoming challenger and the need for protection.

Then it's time to consider how to apply those skills in the correct way *for the actual situation the player is facing*. The type of header will vary not only according to the situation faced but also the part of the field where the header is taking place.

Defensive heading

Normally, the main requirement in a successful defensive headed clearance – in order of importance – are:

1. Height
2. Distance
3. Direction – away from the scoring zone.

Attacking heading

In terms of importance, it is nearly always:

1. Accuracy
2. Power – this gives defenders and goalkeeper little time to recover.

Midfield

The middle section of a soccer field is always "disputed territory". Midfield players must, first of all, fight to deny the opposition the ball, and then, better still, gain possession for themselves. Once successful, they should use that possession to create attacking positions. These factors are reflected in midfield heading.
Priority 1. Challenge to deny opposition a clear header.
Priority 2. Win the ball in the air against opposition.
Priority 3. Direct header to a team mate to maintain possession.

Deflection heading

Deflection heading takes place when the direction of a ball is changed without imparting any further pace on the ball. It is very beneficial in midfield to direct an aerial ball to the feet of a team mate. It can also be valuable in attacking situations, particularly those involving the scoring zone where, for example, a cross can be deflected at the near post away and past a goalkeeper and/or defenders into the net, or deflected into the path of a team mate who strikes for goal.

The thrill of a superb header is not reserved exclusively for the performer. It gladdens the heart of a coach, and always brings shouts of acclaim from team mates and soccer fans.

Chapter 6
DRIBBLING OR RUNNING WITH THE BALL

SECTION I

Give a toddler a soccer ball and encourage him to kick it, and you can guarantee that he will. What's more, he will then run after the ball and kick it again and again! It is the most natural instinct in the game. By kicking and running with the ball, a youngster is "dribbling", albeit in a fairly basic way. One of the worst things a soccer coach can do is discourage young players from dribbling because it is "more important" to pass the ball. **It is not more important to pass the ball**. There are times when passing is the best thing to do. There are other times when dribbling past a defender will greatly increase the attacking possibilities for a team.

Running with the ball past opponents is one of the most exciting and admired skills in the game. The action of beating just one defender can destroy defensive tactics, unnerve opponents and give confidence to one's own team mates. It is a skill to be encouraged and practised, not frowned upon. Young players in particular should be allowed to learn

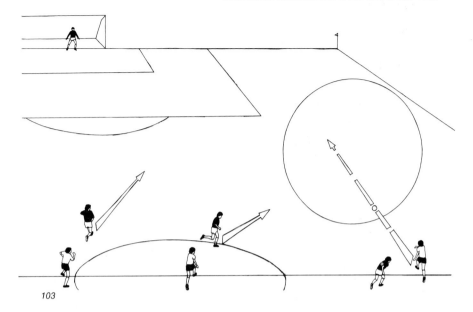

103

when it is best to dribble in a game and when it would be more appropriate to cross or pass. **Don't let young players think they are doing something wrong by taking on defenders.** Even though the game is 11 against 11, nothing is more thrilling and meaningful than the one versus one challenge. The action of one player can change the whole course of the game – the difference between winning and losing. However, there are a number of important considerations that a player running with the ball needs to keep in mind in terms of dribbling skills.

1. *Speed of dribble*

If the space in the attacking half of the field is open, with no defender in the immediate vicinity to contend with, the player "on the ball" should play it forward as far as he can without risking its loss. He then should run as fast as he can after the ball before defenders can recover and reposition. It's a case of "hit and run" (see *illustration 103*). Most times, however, there is a marking defender nearby so the ball must be kept under fairly close control. In such a situation, the objective must be to unbalance the defender – so that he cannot do his job properly – by taking it at him, or past him. This can often be achieved by a *change of pace*. For example, **slow and slow and then quick** – may leave the defender standing. **Quick and quick – and then a check to slow** may leave him stumbling. The ability to stop stone dead is a very useful tool that may well send a defender staggering clumsily away.

104

105

2. Change of direction

A short change of direction can also unbalance the defender (see *illustrations 104 and 105*). **In and then out, or out and then in and out again**, plus a *change of pace*, may be the successful formula. There are many combinations.

3. Manipulating the ball

Dragging the ball sideways, backwards, sometimes with the sole or the inside or outside of the foot (see *illustrations 106 and 107*) can bemuse defenders and cause them to make uncontrolled challenges, ultimately kicking thin air. Often, a flick of the ball over the challenging defender's outstretched leg will be enough for the player with the ball to skip out of the challenge and leave the defender floundering, hopelessly beaten.

106

107

4. Faking

Faking to "trick" an opponent is another important tool of the dribbling trade. Faking can be achieved by body movement without necessarily manipulating the ball:

1. A dip of the shoulder
2. Threatening to kick the ball
3. Pretending to go one way, and moving another
4. Playing the foot over the ball.

The fake is normally followed by an incisive action. For example, after faking to go one way, the player plays the ball and moves at pace in another direction.

108

5. Cat-and-mouse

The dribbler needs to be in control of *himself and the ball* at all times, or there is a good chance he could lose out to the threatening defender who is just waiting for a mistake. At the same time, the dribbler needs to be ready and alert to react to the defender's movements. Once a defender begins to stumble or to tackle, once he is off-balance or unsighted (see *illustration 108*), the dribbler must act *swiftly* and *incisively* to leave the defender "for dead". So **alertness, awareness, confidence and the knowledge of your own ability are valuable qualities here**.

6. Screening

Screening is the act of keeping the ball away from a challenging player by putting some part of the body between the ball and the challenger (see *illustration 109*) so that he cannot win the ball. It is a necessary skill for any position on the field. Defenders, in possession, sometimes

109

110

111

need to use this skill when caught around their own penalty area and unable for that moment to "clear their lines". Strikers must be able to screen in and around the attacking penalty area to prevent defenders from blocking or tackling them as they manoeuvre for a shooting position. Wing players use screening while dribbling forward to deny defenders the opportunity to win the ball. But there is another important function of screening: placing some part of the body between the ball and the challenger can affect the defender's ability to see the ball. Losing sight of the ball often forces defenders to act hastily and foolishly as they try to regain control of the situation. That split second of "lost vision" becomes the time to fool the defender with some explosive dribbling action (see *illustrations 110 and 111*).

7. The combination

The six factors we've just discussed need to be brought together, and this can only be achieved by the player himself. All require practice, and the following pages will provide appropriate exercises and practice games. But when all is said and done – and practised! – it is the player himself, with some help from his coach, who will have to decide just where his strengths lie and how he can best use those abilities. No player in the world is perfect at everything. Successful players are those who can adapt their particular strengths to a given situation in the very best way.

Practice 1

The practice run is set out as shown in *illustration 112*. Cones should be placed carefully. I suggest two yards between each cone, although a few inches either way will not make any difference as long as they are *exactly* the same distance each time you practise. You might want to use a broom handle to mark the exact distance between each one. You will see why in a moment. A variety of different runs can be practised – all will greatly help a player's ability to run with and manipulate the ball while at the same time keeping it under tight control. Here are just a few of the runs:

1. Starting from the end, zigzag through the cones, around the top cone and back to the starting line.
2. Sprint to the top cone with the ball, back to the middle cone, make a complete circle of the middle cone, and then return to the goal line.

112

113

3. Using your imagination, and the cones, as an obstacle course, go in and out of the cones wherever you choose, throwing in two or three tricks or fakes at any time.

4. Go from the starting cone to the middle cone, make a complete turn, then move up to the top cone, make another complete circle, back to the middle cone, a complete circle there, and return to the starting cone.

You can time yourself on runs 1, 2, and 4 and keep a record, always hoping to beat your best time. That is the reason to make sure the practice run is exactly the same each time. Don't time run 3 like the others – just use it to practise and experiment. Let your imagination really go wild and try all kinds of different tricks and fakes.

Don't forget to use both feet. Even keep a record to see how well you perform on your less comfortable foot.

When practising with friends, make it competitive by seeing who has the best time, or mark out a second practice run with exactly the same distances and race against one another.

Practice 2

Practice 2 is a one versus one game. The area size is approximately 20 yards x 10 yards (see *illustration 113*), with goals four feet wide. If the goals are too wide, it becomes too easy to score; if too narrow, one player could simply stand in front of his own goal and make it almost impossible to score.

The game is very simple: the idea is to score, but to do that, the player with the ball will either have to beat his opponent, or at the very least move him off the line to goal so that a shot can be made. Whichever method is used, the defending player will have to be faked to move him out of a good defending position. When the ball goes out of play, it is restarted by the player who didn't touch it last, and is dribbled in from the point at which the ball left the field. The opponent must be at least five yards away from the point of entry.

You will find the game hard work, so don't be afraid to take time-outs. If there are three or four of you, take turns and play three-goals-in for each game.

Practice 3
Shooting and defence

Here is a fine game I used to play for hours as a youngster – many years ago! A minimum of three players is required, although four to five can be accommodated in the same game. *Illustration 114* shows an actual soccer field being used, but a similar area can be set up anywhere there is space approximately the size of a penalty area, or even a little smaller. The goalkeeper starts the game by throwing the ball out towards the edge of the area. Whichever of the players is the first to the ball becomes the attacker, looking to score a goal. The defender tries to stop the attacker – or better still, gains possession of the ball from the attacker, at which point *he* becomes the attacker. One moment, a player

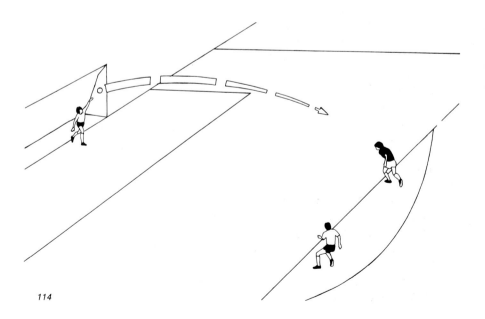

114

is an attacker; the next, if he loses the ball, a defender. As well, a player can pick up a rebound from the goalkeeper and score, even though he may not have been the one who shot at goal. So everyone must be on the alert until a goal is scored, or at least until the ball goes out of play.

The problem with having more than three players is that one player could be tempted to cheat and hover around the goal area, looking for easy rebound goals without working for them.

The first player to score three goals is the winner. He then chooses who will go in goal: either himself – if he wants to have a rest or practise his goalkeeping – or another player, but not the existing goalkeeper. Goalkeepers should not be forced to stay in for more than one round unless they themselves are prepared to do so.

This game will lead to many one versus one situations in the penalty area, requiring the attacker to try to go past a defender, or at least move him off the line to goal in order to create a shooting opportunity for himself.

𝄞 𝄞 SECTION II

The parent/coach can be the hero or the villain when it comes to dribbling. He can discourage a player's inclination to dribble, or he can encourage and help develop this most exciting and vital aspect of the game. I urge you to adopt the latter approach. Don't be too concerned about "coaching", either – just give a youngster a challenging opportunity to practise running with the ball and throw in some "soft" suggestions, rather than "hard" instructions.

Practices 1, 2 and 3 of Section I will all benefit from the coach's organisation and supervision. Certainly use Practice 1 on a regular

115

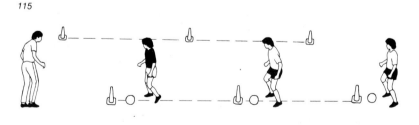

basis, and set out a run for each youngster if you can. This will allow races to take place. Or ask each player individually to do his own thing. If you wish, you can award marks out of 10 as they do in figure skating and gymnastics, after players have each completed their run. Their creativity may surprise you. There may be a few lighter moments when a youngster becomes over-ambitious, but beware of stifling a young player's experimentation through ridicule.

Practice 4

Another worthwhile variation of Practice 1 is shown in *illustration 115*. Three lines are marked, three to four yards apart, with markers on the side lines. Each player starts on the centre line with a ball. The coach stands facing the players and gives instructions. For instance, he can shout "right" or "left", "this way" or "that way", and point in the appropriate direction. He may substitute "right" and "left" with other code words such as "north and south" or "dog and cat".

Or he may simply tell the players that they will be going to the right or the left on the word "go", and so not try to trick the youngsters in this instance.

The course can be varied by the coach. His instructions might be, "around the outside cone and back, with the ball stone dead on the centre line"; "around the outside cone, all the way across to the other cone, make a complete circle with the ball and back to the centre line"; or "first one with the ball stone dead on the outside line – go!" Points are given for each winner and a running total is kept. More than two players – in fact, a whole team – can be accommodated in such a practice if the coach's organisation is effective. With large numbers you may have to operate without cones.

Practice 5

If you can find a soccer field for this practice, so much the better. It will be very meaningful to the young player. As you can see from *illustrations 116 and 117*, a "corridor" has been set up (20 yards x 10 yards) out on the flanks of the field. If the field is too wide for the age of the players, bring the corridor in and create an imaginary touch line as in the illustration. The coach passes the ball to the attacker who starts in the opposite corner of the corridor to the defender. As soon as the ball is played, however, the defender can move in to challenge. The attacker cannot cross the ball until he has moved out of the corridor from the end line. He should then attempt to make a successful cross into the penalty area, althouth the player does not have to cross the ball as soon

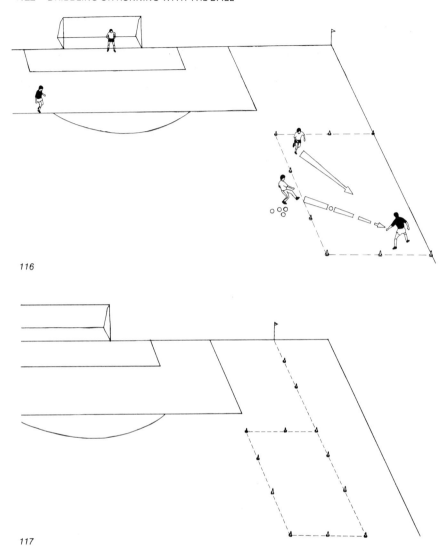

116

117

as he moves over the line. He may continue to work the ball and the defender in order to create the right sort of opening. But he *cannot cross the ball* **before** coming out of the corridor. Numbers will dictate whether there will be a goalkeeper and players attacking the cross in the penalty area. Use targets at the near and far post if there are insufficient players to attack the cross. (Go back and review Chapter 4 on Crossing to get the most out of this practice.)

To turn the practice into a competitive, one versus one game, the attacker is given two points every time he cleanly beats the defender, and two points for every "good" cross; the defender receives one point for every successful tackle or unsuccessful attempted cross.

Practice 6

Illustration 118 shows a one versus one on the edge of the penalty area. The ability to beat defenders in an effort to create openings for a shot at goal is an important requirement for an attacking player, and a vital part of dribbling and running with the ball. In this practice, the coach plays to the attacker who must work to create a scoring opportunity. The defender and the goalkeeper do whatever they can – within the rules – to prevent the attacker from scoring. The coach can serve the ball in from a variety of angles – the illustration shows merely one example. The practice can be made competitive by changing around the attacker, the

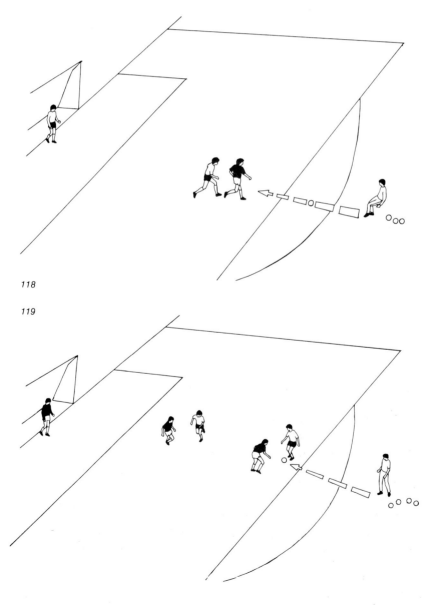

118

119

defender and the goalkeeper after so many attempts on goal. The winner is the player who scores the most times.

If there are five players available, progress the exercise into a two versus two with the same basic organisation (*illustration 119*) but only after practising the one versus one first. The extra advantage of two versus two is that players can "combine" together to produce a strike at goal. There will still be ample opportunity to beat a defender and so make an opening for a shot. But the presence of other alternatives – a short pass for a shot or a one-two (give and go) – will help make the practice just that bit more realistic.

SECTION III

One of the least commendable characteristics of soccer coaches the world over is their tendency to discourage the dribbler and to dismiss individualism because it is "anti-team" or because "soccer is a passing game". The objective of soccer is to put the ball into the scoring zone, and from there to score goals. The means to that end are many; the ball can be moved from one end of the field to the other by passing or by simply running with it. Most likely, it will be a combination of the two. It is a fact, however, that in most circumstances, **dribbling and running with the ball is more effective in the attacking half of the field than in the defending half.** That *does not* mean players should not run with the ball in their defending half, nor is it necessarily wrong to dribble past an opponent in your own penalty area. But if possession is lost in the defending half of the field, the dangers created will obviously be far greater.

What I am suggesting is that you emphasise to players the *most productive* areas of the field in which to beat a player with a ball, and so encourage them to do just that.

They are:

1. *In and around the attacking penalty area:* Beating a player here usually gives a very real chance of a shot at goal, so that taking the gamble of losing the ball in this situation is worthwhile.

2. *Out on the flanks in the attacking half:* Beating a defender out on the wings will throw the defending team into a state of confusion. As a dribbling player makes progress down the wing, all defenders are forced to retreat back towards their own goal which will not please them! They will then have to decide whether to send one or more defenders out to the wings to help repel the attacker. By doing so, they will leave the scoring zone poorly defended. But if defenders elect to stay in

120

the central defending area, they then concede to the dribbling player the advantage of crossing – under no pressure at all – or of moving in towards the goal with a chance of scoring himself.

I trust you will now look on the technique of dribbling with new respect. No one will deny that dribbling in your own penalty area can pose great dangers. Sometimes, however, a player has no alternative. Point out the risks of losing the ball in those areas of the field, but at the same time emphasise the great advantages of taking players on in the attacking half.

In reviewing earlier sections of this chapter, keep in mind that Practices 1, 2, 4, 5 and 6 can all be adapted to the team practice.

Practice 7

This is an introductory, fun activity for dribbling but you need one ball per player. The idea is for each player to keep possession of his own ball in the prescribed area, while at the same time trying to kick all other balls out of the area (see *illustration 120*). Once a ball goes out of the area, its "owner" is eliminated and drops out of the practice. Eventually, two players are left for the final challenge to decide the winner.

Another way of conducting the same practice is for everyone to have a ball except one person – the "destroyer". His task is to eliminate everybody, one by one. In this version, those with the ball do not attempt to kick another ball away, but do everything possible to keep their own ball away from the destroyer.

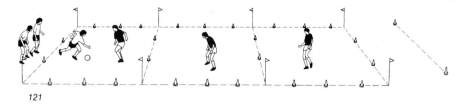

121

Practice 8

The squad is divided into groups of six, and split three versus three. As you can see in *illustration 121*, three squares are set up, each measuring 10 yards x 10 yards. The defending side is positioned one in each square, and there each player must remain. The three attacking players outside the starting square each have a ball. The object is for each player to dribble the ball through the three squares and finish with it stone dead on the line beyond the squares, but it is not permitted to go beyond that line with the ball and then return back. That specific rule prevents players from kicking the ball firmly through the final square. One point is scored for every square that a player successfully "navigates" – this allows a maximum three points per player, nine points per team. When all three have completed their turn, the teams change with the defending team now attacking and vice versa.

The coach chooses from two alternative methods of play:

1. Players go singly, with the next man able to take a turn only when his team mate has completed his attempt.
2. Each team may decide on its own strategy: players can go at the same time, or singly, or whatever – **and they don't have to let the opposition know!**

This type of practice requires careful planning – and particularly with a large group.

Practice 9

Illustration 122 shows a six-a-side game where the field has been split into two, with two attackers versus three defenders and a goalkeeper situation in each half. For the two attackers to be successful against the three defenders, they are virtually compelled to take chances because of the odds against them. They should be encouraged to take on the

defenders. The goalkeeper and the defenders, having gained possession of the ball, attempt to pass to their two attackers in the other half of
the field. But they must be careful to give their attackers a chance to
receive the ball in a good position, to enable them to then strike at the
opposing goal. The attacking players are allowed to play the ball back
across the half-way line to their team mates, and this opportunity
should be taken advantage of when they are tightly marked and looking
for another chance to break loose from the markers.

The two attackers will probably find it difficult to make openings for
themselves, but they should still be encouraged to do so, as this is a
very realistic situation in the game. Whenever a player creates an opening for a shot, it should be acknowledged and his play complimented,
even if he does not score.

Practice 10
The man-marking game

Page 305 in "The Games Soccer Players Play" section describes in
detail how the man-marking game is organised, and what its benefits
are. In Practice 10, the game is used to emphasise dribbling. The man-
marking game will also make attacking players aware of their co-
operating team mates who can offer them the alternative of passing,
particularly when a colleague off-the-ball has not received the close
attention of his marker. With a large group, the man-marking game can
be combined with change-soccer to keep everyone involved.

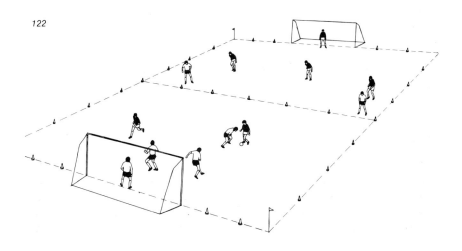

122

Summary

Practices 8 and 9 need careful planning, plus the availability of the right kind of facilities and equipment. Don't be concerned if it is not a practical possibility or if you are a little unsure of yourself. The practices in Sections I and II, when adapted to the team session, together with Practices 7 and 10 will provide plenty of simple yet effective dribbling workouts.

Now, as one of my old coaches used to say at the end of his pre-game talk, "OK, boys, go out and get after them". That meant our using a number of different techniques – including, thankfully, the great skill of dribbling.

Chapter 7
HUSTLING AND TACKLING

 SECTION 1

Introduction

Various terms are used to describe the act of defending in a one versus one situation. Players are encouraged to "close down" the player with the ball, which means that standing off some five or six yards invites the attacking player to run at the defender and turn him inside out. This he will probably do if he comes at speed. Therefore, a defender should "close him down" – or "pressurise" him – or "hustle" him – so that the attacker has little or no time to compose himself. In North America, the skill is more commonly termed "hustling"; in Europe, "jockeying" or "pressurising". Whatever, the jockeying and tackling of players – very much a one versus one situation, even in the 11-a-side game – is the subject we will now deal with.

My fellow coach back in Liverpool, Ronnie Moran, remarked that "they spoiled the game of soccer when they introduced opposition".

123   124

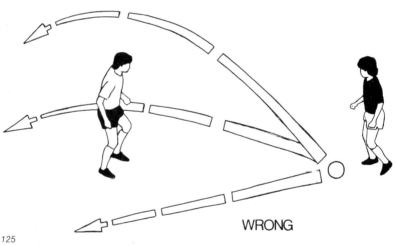

WRONG

125

Ronnie had a point. Scoring, passing, shooting and crossing would all be so much easier *without opposition*. It is the opponents who stop things from happening. Opponents simply won't do as they are told! They refuse to co-operate. And here lies the strength of the defender. **He should do everything the attacker wishes him not to do.**

Defenders who show **patience, composure and discipline** will be difficult to beat. But more than just those three qualities are required: defenders need defending skill.

Hustling

Ideally, a hustling player should be within striking distance of the player with the ball. The slightest error in judgement on the part of the attacking player should give the defender the opportunity to win the ball. Therefore, he needs to be close, but not so close that he cannot see the ball beneath him, nor so far away that the pressure is taken off the attacker. A distance of approximately four to six feet is ideal. Refer to *illustrations 123 and 124*. However, if the defender is more than six feet away from the attacking player with the ball as in *illustration 125* the pressure is less intense and the attacker can play the ball past the defender, bend the ball around him, or run at him and have the defender stumbling backwards. If the defender is more than three yards away, the ball can be easily played over the defender.

Balanced position – "Ready for action"

When we discussed dribbling, it was suggested that the best way to overcome a defender was to "unbalance" him, or make him lose control of himself. In order to avoid this, the defender must take up a "balanced" and alert, "ready-for-any-action" position, as shown in *illustration 126*. The defender stands on the balls of his feet, not on his heels.

126

127

128

His nose and eyes are pointing towards the ball – why should a defender watch anything else in a one versus one? One leg is in front of the other, and the body is half-turned (*illustration 127*) (a square position tends to put the player "on his heel" and also invites the attacker to go either way). See *illustration 128*. Thus, in a half-turned position, the defender is "encouraging" the attacker to go the way *he* would like him to go – not necessarily the way the attacker would like to go. In this respect, the defender influences the decisions of the attacker as much as possible. See *illustrations 129, 130 and 131*.

129

130

131

From this balanced, poised, snake-like position, the defender is ready to bite – *if he wants to*. It is crucial, however, that the defender be prepared for any decision the attacker may make. **Remember, the attacker has the ball and, no matter what the "influence", he is able to make his own choice – good or bad.** So the defender must assume nothing and be prepared for anything, while continuing to attempt to influence the attacker's decision. The hustling position, explained thus far, gives the defender that preparedness.

A defending player should remember that once an opponent has received a ball and is running at him, it is much more difficult to achieve the ideal, well-balanced hustling position. All the more reason for being alert and trying to close down the attacker before he has time to control the ball. Sometimes, however, that is not possible. With space between the defending player and the attacker, and the opportunity for the attacker to run at his opponent, the defender must still close him down – but more cautiously and gradually, always with the objective of eventually "engaging" the attacker four to six feet away.

Having achieved a good hustling or jockeying position, there are three major ways of winning the ball.

1. The steal

Through a close challenge position, a player is able to threaten the dribbler – even fake a tackle – which may cause the attacker to lose full control of the ball. This will present an opportunity for the ball to be "stolen" without the necessity of a full-blooded tackle. The steal and the block tackle (explained next) emphasise the importance of closing down opponents to within the four-to six-foot range. How can you steal a ball if you are four yards away?

2. The block tackle

This is the basic tackle that all players should learn. *Illustrations 132, 133 and 134* show a strong block tackle that incorporates the following essential ingredients:

a. The tackler should be composed and well-balanced when moving aggressively in to challenge. Lunging forward must be avoided as this will give the attacker in possession time to take avoiding action.
b. The non-tackling foot is placed slightly to one side and slightly behind the ball.

132

133

134

135   136

c. As contact is made with the ball, the whole of the body goes into the challenge. The striking action is aggressive but controlled and, at the moment of impact, the momentum should not go through the ball (see *illustration 134*). Instead, a strong position is held momentarily, and then the ball is "squeezed" out and past the dribbling player by the power of the challenging player.

The block tackle will usually take place in two different situations: as the final challenge for the ball after hustling the attacker into a favourable position, or as a one versus one disputed challenge for an unclaimed ball – from a clearance or misplaced pass, for example.

The circumstances will be different in each case but the block tackle techniques remain the same.

3. The slide tackle

Sometimes the hustling circumstances are not all that the defender would wish – you'll recall my remarks about attacking players having the space to run at defenders. Even in a good hustling position, the attacker still has the ball and can, therefore, make the decision. If an attacking player goes past a defender and the defender is unable to steal or block tackle, all is not lost. The slide tackle may at times be a little desperate, but it can also be most effective (see *illustrations 135, 136, 137, 138 and 139*).

137

138

139

The best time to slide tackle is when an attacker has taken on a defender and gained a half-yard advantage, or on a run to goal on a through-ball. To give himself a good chance of making a successful challenge, the defender must not slide desperately into the tackle. Instead, he must run hard to maintain the threatening position by the side of the dribbling player, **and then pick his moment to slide forward alongside the attacking player and strike the ball away** (preferably out of play) **from the attacker** (*illustrations 135, 136, 137 and 138*). For an effective sweeping tackle, use the leg furthermost from the attacker. This will become the upper leg in the sliding position, and the sweeping movement is best executed using this leg (see *illustration 139*).

There are obvious risks involved in the slide tackle and they must be taken into account:

a. If the defender misses the ball, he is left on the ground and out of the game.

b. If the defender successfully plays the ball and it stays inside the field of play, he is still at a disadvantage because of the time taken to get back on his feet.

c. If the defender misses the ball but connects with the attacker, he concedes a free kick or – if the incident occurs in the penalty area – a penalty which means an almost certain goal.

Risks notwithstanding, the slide tackle is still a very necessary defensive skill.

Practice 1

On your own, using a wall or similar solid surface, practise the block tackle technique (see *illustration 140*).

The wall won't yield, but it *will* help you practice the timing and mechanics of the block tackle. Start approximately four to six feet away and step into the block tackle strongly with a one-two movement, then

140

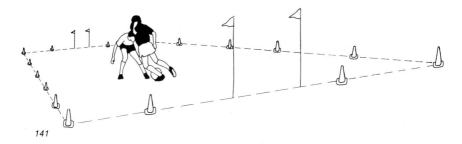

141

squeeze the ball into the wall. Remember, you cannot complete the block tackle as you are not able to push through the final part of the challenge. Don't even try, as you might injure yourself. Keep in mind, however, the need to add the final part when you apply the block tackle in an actual game.

Practice 2
One versus one with goals

This is the same exercise as Practice 2 in Chapter 6, Dribbling. In soccer, one skill often gives the opponent practice in the corresponding opposite skill, as in this case. Here is a one versus one game (consult page 118 for the rules) in which the player not in possession must defend very well and very patiently, or he could make it relatively easy for his opponent to score (see *illustration 141*).

Practice 3

This is the shooting and defence practice of the last chapter (see Chapter 6, Practice 3, for the organisation and rules). I would strongly

142

143

recommend this game to give first-class practice in hustling and tack-ling. From two to five players can participate in this exercise (see *illustration 142*).

Practice 4

This hustling practice begins with two lines drawn approximately 20 yards apart. The player with the ball tries to get past the other and to the opposite line (see *illustration 143*). The hustling player must stay close to the player with the ball, four to six feet away, and should work hard not to let the dribbler twist and turn him one way and then the other. The golden rule is that the defender should *never* be turned completely round or he will lose both his balance and the sight of the ball – one is as bad as the other.

The hustling player in this practice is not permitted to tackle, so he must hustle extremely well to keep the attacker in front of him. After reaching the 20-yard line, players change roles with the defender, then attacking on the return journey. This is an exercise rather than a game, but one that should be repeated often – say, five minutes, twice a week.

SECTION II

In working with youngsters on hustling and tackling techniques, the parent/coach must provide both encouragement and inspiration – in hefty doses. For most players, there are obviously more exciting and enjoyable aspects of the game. But I appeal to the coach to resist the temptation to neglect these essential defensive skills.

Practice 5
One forward/one back

This is a drill that may not be as entertaining as the other game formats in the book, but is truly worthwhile for the practice it provides.

Four players are required – if there are only three, the coach must join

144

in! Two lines are drawn, approximately 15 to 20 yards apart (see *illustration 144*). The objective is exactly the same as in Practice 4 of Section I, and this is the way it should be set up if there are only two players. Initially there must be three players at one end, one with the ball. Player 1 starts with the ball. He is marked by Player 2 and the sequence runs as follows: 1 dribbles the ball at 2 who jockeys Player 1 while retreating backwards across to the other side. Once at the other side, 1 taps the ball to Player 3 who then runs the ball at 1 – now the defender – on the return journey, Player 2 having dropped out. At the other side, Player 4 replaces 1, with Player 3 returning as the defender and so on. Each sequence should last from about 90 seconds to two minutes, and then the players earn a rest.

Defenders should keep the following points in mind:

1. Get down with knees bent and nose pointing towards the ball.
2. On your toes, with the body weight on the balls of the feet.
3. Try not to be twisted one way, then the other.
4. Instead, attempt to influence the attacker by staying half-turned and forcing the attacker one way only – down the side of the defender.

145

Because this is a defensive drill and not a game, don't spend too long on this practice. Two minutes, then a one-minute rest, then another two minutes of practice – five minutes in total – will be ample.

Practice 6
Spin and go

This is another drill rather than a game, but a challenging one that will bring out players' competitive instincts through the one versus one situation.

Illustration 145 shows a group of four players, with two lines marked 20 yards apart. The players at either end each have a ball. The two players in the middle are designated either attacker or defender. In this case the defender is Player 1 who must aim to keep the attacker Player 2 in a closely marked hustling position at all times. The attacker tries to shake off the defender by faking one way or the other. The attacker's objective is to call for a pass from one of the servers, receive it, and play it back (one-touch or two-touch) to the same server, having lost the defender.

The rules allow the attacker to receive the ball only when he actually *asks* for it from one of the servers. The defender must attempt to stay with the attacker at all times and not be faked – by remaining on what would, in a game, be the "goal side" in relation to where the attacker is running. The defender's objective is not to tackle but to stay in a close hustling position. Victory for the attacking player is achieved when he receives the ball from a server with the defender "missing" – that is, not in a close hustling position. The ultimate success for the attacker, however, is to have faked the defender so well that he falls over.

A sustained effort of 30 to 45 seconds per pair is sufficient: any longer will reduce the exercise to an endurance test and that is not the idea. The idea is for the defender to work skilfully to maintain a balanced, close, marking position without tackling. Make sure the roles of each pair are reversed alternately so that each player has a turn at attacking.

SECTION III

Practice 7

Practice 7 is a one versus one game. Instead of one goal to defend, each player has two (see *illustration 146*). This forces a rapid adjustment of the hustling position when the player on the ball seeks to change his point of attack to score in the alternative goal. The goals should be no more than one yard in width to make it relatively difficult to score. The

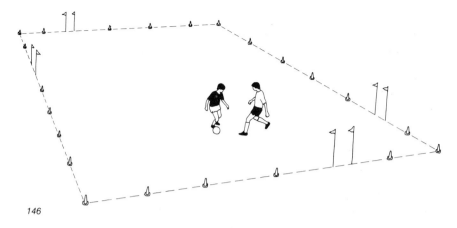

146

attacker has to work hard to trick his opponent, and so off-balance him to gain the opportunity of scoring. The game is very demanding physically, so if you are working with four players, use the change-soccer principle outlined in Chapter 1. Organise additional similar areas for the other players.

The team coach should provide clear and precise instruction on hustling techniques. I recommend a careful review of the description set out in Section I to begin with. And as with the demonstration of new skills, proceed at a comfortable pace. It is better to first set up practices which compel players to hustle well – or suffer the consequences – such as practices 2, 5, 6 and 7, then adapt these to the team session with careful preparation and organisation. In defending, one thing is certain: if players consistently lay off attackers, they will defend poorly. Therefore, players should be encouraged to get close whenever the circumstances allow.

Practice 8

Practice 8 is a further adaptation of Practice 8 in Chapter 6. Read that Practice again now to understand the basic organisation and scoring system.

The main difference here is that a sanctuary corridor (see *illustration 147*) is put in between the 10-yard squares to enable each attacking

147

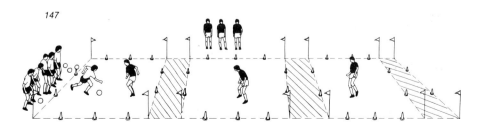

player to compose himself before attacking the next defender. To be completely successful, an attacker must finish with the ball stone dead under his control in the final shaded sanctuary. By doing so, he scores the maximum three points. Once the field is in place, the rest of the organisation is simple: split the group in two, with half attacking and the other half taking turns in defending. With an exceptionally large group – numbers over 14 – you may have to consider setting up a second practice field. Make sure, as coach, that you keep careful score, as this game will be fiercely contested! Just be careful it is not too fierce!

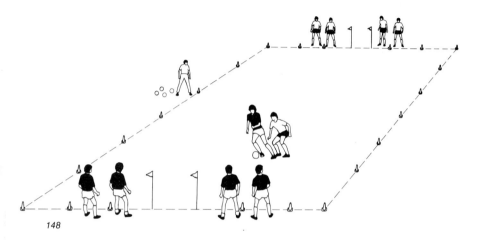

148

Practice 9
The numbers game

Practice 9 shows a 20 yard x 10 yard soccer field with small goals approximately four feet wide (see *illustration 148*). The field size can be adjusted according to players' age and size. In this example, two teams of five are arranged at each end. Each player on each team is given a number from one to five. The coach rolls a ball onto the field – he can bias the service any way he wishes – and shouts out a number. Let's use three as an example. The three's of each team come out to play in a one versus one situation, and try to score a goal. If the ball is kicked out of the practice area, the coach can either roll another ball for the same two to continue – especially if they have only been "in" for a few seconds – or direct the players back behind the goal line, ready for the next numbers to be shouted out. No player off the field is allowed to stand between the goals, nor put a foot out to stop a goal from rolling in. Should that happen, a penalty is awarded – a free shot from the centre of the field without a goalkeeper. Similarly, if a number is shouted – for example, two – and one of the two's fails to come out, or a wrong "number" comes out, a penalty is awarded against the offending team.

Chapter 11 deals with defensive supporting play, and in it, this practice game will be developed into two versus two, and three versus three situations using the same principles. But for now, the coach should concentrate on improving hustling and tackling techniques in a one versus one situation. Don't be tempted to progress the practice too early, but you may want to take a look at Chapter 11, Practice 8, to understand the potential progression.

Denying space, as we will see in Chapter 11, is the basis of defensive tactics, but most defensive strategies are undermined if one player is easily and consistently beaten, or if one or more players will not move in to engage the opposition. That is why the one versus one is of fundamental importance and must be practised regularly.

Chapter 8
CONTROLLING THE BALL

🏐 SECTION I

Good ball control – the skill involved in taking the pace off a pass (or a cross, a clearance, even a shot for that matter) – brings with it many advantages. Above all, it buys time and so gives the *space* necessary to do the next thing. The quicker the ball is "killed" and under the player's control, the less opportunity there is for an opponent to "dispute" possession. Practice is the key to the acquisition of control. Ball control, as I have pointed out, doesn't apply just to passing. Controlling clearance kicks, shots and crosses are just as important and often more difficult, but the principles are the same.

In any type of ball control, whether it be with the foot, the thigh or the chest, there are certain processes that have to be followed.

1. Move into the ball's line of flight

One of the most fundamental considerations for a goalkeeper is to try to get as much of the body behind the ball as possible. The same applies to ball control. If it is possible to move into the path of the ball early, then more of the body can be used to make contact with the ball and so reduce the risk of a mis-control.

2. Move to or away from the ball

If an opponent is coming in to challenge, or is attempting to intercept the ball, it may be necessary to move towards the ball even when a pass is coming in hard and fast. On the other hand, a player may have enough time to move away in order to increase the chances of a good contact, or even to move away from an opponent coming towards the controlling player – that is, not marking from behind.

When moving away from, rather than to, a pass it is best not to use the "move into the line of flight" rule quite as rigidly. Actually *being* in the line of flight while moving away may result in losing sight of the ball. The trick in this case is to run in a line to the side of the line of flight of the ball, until the time comes to make the controlling contact (see *illustration 149*).

3. Choose the controlling surface

While moving into the line of flight, and having decided whether to move forwards or backwards, a further vital decision must be made at the earliest possible stage – **which part of the body is to be used to control the ball?** Hands are out! So it will probably be the foot, the thigh or the chest. Sometimes the stomach is used, or the head. But the head is an extremely difficult surface to control the ball with – for your

149

own use, anyway. You can, of course, take the pace off the ball with your head by deflecting it towards one of your own players. We will look at the specific controlling surfaces and the methods of controlling the ball a little later. But the choice of which surface is to be used becomes crucial as the body has to be "shaped" in order to accept the ball for control.

150

151

4. To cushion or to wedge?

The wedge trap can be used with the foot and, in the case of a bouncing ball, with the stomach (see *illustrations 150 and 151*). The problem with the wedge is that it often takes an extra touch either to complete the control or to set the ball up for the ensuing pass. The most widely used controlling method is that of taking the pace off the ball by a cushioning effect, in which case the surface is presented to the ball and withdrawn at the moment of contact to kill its momentum.

5. Where to control?
Controlling the ball to
where you want it

The final basic consideration, while points 1 to 4 are being put into action, is to decide *where* the ball is to be controlled *to* – so that it can be used to best advantage, or at least protected from the opposition. Several factors should be kept in mind:

    a. The ball should be controlled and kept close to the body but not in a position where a defender can steal, intercept, or tackle (see *illustration 152*). The ball is shielded from a challenging opponent.
    b. However, if the next touch is to be a pass, the ball should be controlled in such a way that the ball position is set up for the pass without the time-consuming necessity of another touch.

152

c. If the player intends to control and dribble past an opponent, the ball needs to be controlled in a position relative to where the opponent is and the direction in which the controlling player wants to run. The decision will be very much influenced by the exact positions of opponents.

Now, let us focus on the more common types of ball control.

1. Foot control

There are four main ways of controlling the ball with the foot:

a. *Side of the foot:* If the fundamentals mentioned earlier have been observed, this is the simplest and most successful of the foot con-

153

154   155

trols (see *illustration 153*). As you can see, the foot reaches slightly forward to receive the ball and is withdrawn on impact to take the pace off it.

b. *The instep:* The instep is normally used in controlling a ball dropping out of the air. There should be a tendency to "claw" and so use some of the outside of the foot (see *illustrations 154 and 155*). The clawing shape gives a larger, "softer" surface, as well as helping the controlling player take up a good shielding position from a marking opponent.

c. *The outside of the foot:* This method (see *illustration 156*) has a number of advantages. It reduces the chances of an opponent's being able to challenge because of the shielding (screening) position, as the leg reaches forward to accept the ball. It is also a natural position from which to steer the ball to the side of, and behind, the

156

157

158   159   160

challenging opponent – spinning on the opponent at the same time.
d. *Stretching in the air:* Stretching for the ball in the air (see *illustration 157*) is not an action of choice, but one of necessity. It happens when there is not enough time to move into the line of flight of the ball, or when there has been a mis-judgement. It requires suppleness and a very fine touch of the ball. A player can improve his technique by working on such regular stretching exercises as a simple thrown service to simulate the control shown in the illustration. Some of the most memorable goals ever scored have occurred when a player has pulled an "impossible" ball out of the air and shot it into the net, to the utter surprise and delight of many.

2. *Thigh control*

As *illustrations 158, 159 and 160* indicate, the thigh control is very effective and rather simple to execute. The thigh presents a large cushioned area (with muscle) and is relatively close to the foot which, in normal circumstances, gives the ball the second touch. Compare this to the chest, where the ball has to drop down several feet before the second touch. The cushioning action required for the control is merely affected by the thigh. And in a game situation where a player is often marked by an opponent from the back, it becomes difficult for the opponent to challenge for the ball. If he does, he will almost certainly commit a foul.

161

162

163

3. Chest control

This is a valuable method of controlling a ball in the air, particularly when marked from behind, as an opponent cannot easily move around the receiving player. As well, the opponent's vision is screened (see *illustration 161*). But considerable practice is required; the action of withdrawing the controlling surface is much more difficult and less natural with the chest than with the foot or the thigh. The cushioning effect is best achieved with a slight bending of the knees after throwing the chest out at the ball as it arrives. The slab of muscle on the upper part of the chest provides the controlling surface. A player can reinforce this effect by keeping the arms to the side and by turning the wrists outwards at the moment of impact, while at the same time hunching the shoulders a little (see *illustrations 162 and 163*).

If you were to try the chest control action in the quiet of your own room, you might well end up looking like the Hunchback of Notre Dame. Don't despair. Just recap the points mentioned and practise in a relaxed fashion. Do not worry too much at first about the withdrawing action, as the cushion of muscle on the chest will be sufficient to take the pace off the ball without its rebounding too far away.

164

165

Practice 1

When practising on your own, your rebound wall will come in handy again. By throwing and kicking the ball against the wall, a player can bring about all the controls that would occur in a game (see *illustration 164*).

Relaxed practice time in control is essential, but if you do want to concentrate on foot and thigh control under more testing circumstances, review the game explained in Chapter 1, Practice 1. It is an ideal practice, but insist on the two-touch rule where the ball must be controlled before being played back onto the wall.

Practice 2

Here is a fine exercise for at least two players. As *illustration 165* shows, begin with two lines 10 yards apart, and a target in the middle. The simple rules for this straightforward but competitive practice are as follows:

1. One point is scored every time the target is hit.
2. No player can enter no-man's-land – the area between the two lines. The penalty is a free kick for the non-offending player from his line with a stationary ball.
3. Two touches *must be taken* each time the ball comes across no-man's-land.
4. The practice begins with one player rolling the ball over to the other

player who must take the required two touches. No points can be scored on the initial service – the roll across.

5. When a mistake stops the sequence, the erring player rolls the ball across to the other player to start the sequence again.

6. The first to score six points is the winner – or else players can agree on their own points-to-win system.

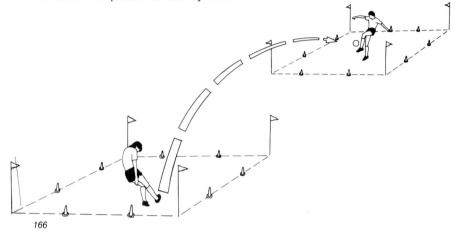

166

Practice 3

Using the same principle as in Practice 2 but removing the target, the two lines can be widened so that lofted, driven and chipped passes are used in practising the chest, thigh and foot controls. Points are conceded for errors committed; the first player to make 10 mistakes is the loser. To eliminate the guesswork, players might want to set an area that the ball must bounce in if allowed. Whenever the ball bounces outside that area, it's clearly an error and the point is conceded (see *illustration 166*).

Practice 4

Illustration 167 shows one player hitting a pass (the distance can vary from 10 to 30 yards) which the second player must accept, no matter

167

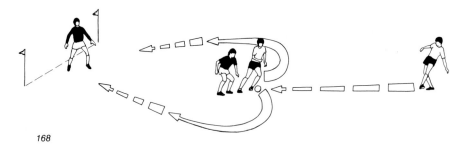

168

what kind of ball comes to him, and turn – or he can do both in the same movement – to fire off a shot at goal. The goals are two yards apart. The marking cones are put in merely as a distraction or as obstacles to be by-passed when turning and shooting. With more than two players, consider using a "live" defender and/or a goalkeeper (see *illustration 168*).

See how many scoring successes can be gained from 10 attempts. Using the two-touch rule, two or three out of 10 without a defender is quite good. One out of 10 with a defender present is not unreasonable but with a "live" defender, use a four-touch maximum rule. High scores won't come easily but steady practice will improve your skills.

🌀🌀 SECTION II

The parent/coach can make a tremendous contribution to the practices of ball control by supplying the right kind of service – by hand or by foot – and by "painting a picture" to stimulate the imagination of young players. In fact, a key phrase for a soccer coach should be *stimulate and simulate* – stimulate the player's imagination, and simulate real game situations whenever possible to make practices meaningful and exciting.

Practices 1, 2, 3 and 4 of Section I can all be modified and enlivened by the coach. Who needs the rebound wall of Practice 1 when Dad's around? The practice can be easily changed to have the coach serve the ball into the players positioned behind a line, who must control the ball (one-touch) and pass sharply back to the coach (second touch). The coach varies the type of service, and for inspiration can even award marks out of 10 for each effort – as in championship diving and figure skating.

All young players – nay, all players – need encouragement, particularly when things aren't going too well. The younger the player, the more encouragement the coach should provide.

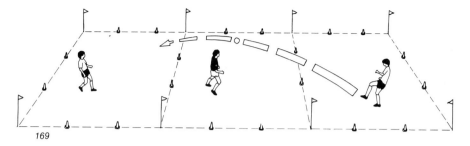

169

Practice 5
Pig-in-the-middle

This practice requires an area as shown in *illustration 169:* three squares, each one approximately 10 yards square. The three players are each confined to their own square. The object is for the two white-shirted players to pass the ball from their own square to the far one. The defender in the middle box tries to intercept, or at least force an error. Once the practice is running smoothly and the "whites" are becoming proficient, you can introduce the condition – three-touch only, or if they are very good, two-touch (see Conditioned Games Section, page 301). Because of the presence of the middle man, the passing player will be encouraged at times to use lofted passes, bringing about frequent opportunities for the chest trap.

The competitive aspect can be introduced by looking for the largest number of consecutive passes without an interception or the ball going out of play. Or see how many passes can be accumulated in three tries. After each sequence, the players are changed from one square to another. The winners can be decided by counting either the greatest number of passes or by selecting whoever keeps the passes to the lowest number – King pig-in-the-middle! This is the same basic practice as Practice 5 of Chapter 2.

Note: You can juggle the size of the practice area – particularly the distance between the outside boxes – to emphasise different types of controls. For example, making the middle box 20 yards long x 10 yards wide instead of 10 x 10 would result in longer passes, lofted balls and different recommendations regarding the type of control that would have to be utilised.

170

Practice 6
Head tennis

The head tennis game is explained more fully in Practice 8, Chapter 5, Heading. The player comes to feel comfortable with the ball while engaging in an enjoyable activity. The game develops touch – so necessary in ball control – and presents many opportunities for control, particularly to the chest and the thigh. Although controlling the ball by keeping it up in the air is not a normal objective in a soccer situation, the principles of controlling in head tennis are closely enough related to make this a most beneficial practice (see *illustration 170*).

 **SECTION III**

Ball control figures prominently in just about every aspect of soccer practice except goalkeeping, so in the normal course of a practice session, every player will have a chance to work on his ball control. However, more formalised practices or game situations are necessary to highlight specific aspects of control. That is, after all, the real purpose of practice – to isolate one part of the game, work at improving that piece of the puzzle and put it back into the big picture so that players can appreciate its relevance and measure what improvement, if any, has taken place.

Practice 7

Here is a simple pairs situation that begins with two lines put in place and a no-man's-land between them which no player can enter (see *illustration 171*). The distance between the lines may be adjusted to

171

encourage specific types of control: distances of 10 yards or less will emphasise short passing on the floor; longer distances of 25 yards or more will emphasise driven and lofted passes resulting in control by chest, thigh and foot. Allow plenty of "free" practice in the beginning so that players can experiment and rehearse without undue pressure. Later, you can introduce a competitive two-touch-only situation. Any player entering no-man's-land is disqualified; the first pair to complete 10 passes wins.

Make sure the distance between the respective pairs is not too close or a misplaced pass or control could unfairly affect another pair's efforts (see *illustration 171*).

Practice 8
Practice A

As *illustration 172* indicates, this practice makes use of a three-square situation – 20 yards square at each end with a 20 x 10 yards rectangle in

172

the middle – but this can be adjusted according to players' age and ability. Three groups of four players are chosen and, as usual, numbers can be adjusted according to how many are at the squad practice. The object is for the four players at one end to keep possession from the one defender. Both groups have a ball each and at first, work separately. The winning group is the one with the highest run of consecutive passes.

After one minute, the resting defenders take over from the active defenders. After the second minute, the four defenders then change with one end group whose members now become the defenders. The practice continues and then there is a final change, with the group that hasn't yet defended taking its turn. Sharp ball control will be vital even in the four versus one, 20-yard square, but as players improve and find it easier to keep the ball away from the one – and that may take 10 weeks, not 10 minutes – a two- or three-touch maximum condition can be imposed.

Practice B

Practice A is then progressed in the following way. Just one ball is used and each group of four works together to keep the ball away from the defenders (the dark-shirted players in the illustration). The objective is to pass the ball from one square to the other. Points are scored for each successful pass. Success *is* judged as playing the ball across the no-man's-land, as long as the ball is accepted and possession retained on the opposite side without a defender intercepting, stealing the pass, or winning the ball in a tackle. However, each group of four must not be too eager to pass across the area if it is likely the ball will be given away. Instead, possession should be maintained in the four versus one until the right opportunity arises to pass across to the other group and so score a point.

The winners are the most successful defending group of four with the least number of consecutive passes against them. The coach can decide on how many turns for each phase or he may choose to set a time limit and switch defenders periodically, the resting pair replacing the active duo.

Practice 9

This practice is a basic three versus three, with two goals (no goal-keepers) two yards wide (see *illustration 173*). Three, as will be emphasised in Chapter 10, is the basic attacking unit. With the three-a-side

173

game conditioned to two-touch maximum, good control – as well as considerate passing and strong support – will be essential to achieve success. The size of the practice area should be adjusted according to players' age and ability, but it is recommended you not make it too "tight" – certainly not until the players become more skilled. Change-soccer rules may be used when working with team squad numbers. It may even be necessary to juggle four versus four, three versus three, or three versus four situations to make sure everyone is involved.

Summary

Controlling the ball – the "first touch" as it's sometimes called – is indeed the essence of soccer, and should be included in *every* session in one form or another. Conditioning the final six-a-side game to two-touch for some part of the game will help enormously (see Games Soccer Players Play, page 301), but players will definitely need specific practices in addition to small-sided games.

What impressed me most about the sport when I first became involved in professional soccer was the remarkable speed with which everything took place. Even as a goalkeeper, I found myself that first season playing games and gasping for breath – and I was in top physical condition. The speed wasn't so much fleetness of foot as the fact that everything was performed so much more rapidly than I was used to. The ball control was so *sharp* that everything else happened half a second faster than in my amateur days.

It was truly breathtaking. So much so that I hardly had time to control myself!

Chapter 9
GOALKEEPING

PART 1

Introduction

Goalkeepers are special soccer people. Mainly, they are handball players and not footballers like the rest of the team. Because of these considerations, this chapter will differ slightly in format from the others. But remember, goalkeepers are "special" only because of the handling requirement. They are very much a part of the team and should not be treated any better or worse than the other players.

There is nothing mystical about goalkeeping. It boils down to a question of understanding the basic skills – and **practice**! There is a saying in soccer that "goalkeepers can be manufactured". In general, I agree with that statement. The goalkeeping task can be approached with almost military precision, though there will always be a need for some heroics, too, to save the day.

A number of years ago, just as I was finishing my playing career as a goalkeeper, I was asked to put on a demonstration of goalkeeping practices for an adult certification course held at the Blackpool Easter School. After the session, there was a discussion among the staff coaches – which I didn't hear about until later – where one of them described my practice suggestions as "too simple, too basic and somewhat naive". He was obviously looking for some complicated formula that would unravel the so-called "mystique" of the goalkeeping art. If I had been in on the conversation, I would have told him very bluntly – there isn't one! And what I suggested that day at Blackpool remains fundamentally the same advice I will give you in this chapter. Let me share with you the same methods that helped me enjoy a successful career, and the same principles that I've used in coaching numerous goalkeepers who have gone onto achieve top-class professional player status.

This chapter will cover the *fundamentals* of goalkeeping. If they are understood and practised, most of the more sophisticated requirements will fall readily into place.

Think of the goalkeeper as the "keeper of the box". The term "keeper" is entirely appropriate as the penalty area can become a bit of a zoo. It becomes something of a crazy, mixed-up zoo, however, when the keeper at times starts to look like the animals. I shall explain shortly why the keeper should act like a leopard, look like a gorilla and perform like an octopus at different times during his goalkeeping duties.

First, lets get...

Ready for action

Before doing anything, a goalkeeper must be ready. If he is not, he won't be able to react immediately. And if split seconds are lost, it could well be too late – except for picking the ball out of the back of the net!

174

1. Body "ready"

Take a good look at *illustration 174*. It shows the goalkeeper "ready for action". He should always be on his toes, fully aware of where the ball is. While the round-shouldered posture of our goalkeeper in the illustration is not recommended off the field, it is a *must* in the "ready" position. If the penalty box is a zoo, then the keeper in this case should be like a caged leopard – always on his toes, constantly moving, watching, ready to pounce.

2. The "open – looking out" position

The keeper needs to view much more than the ball. He must position his body – *at all times* – to enable him to see as much of the field of play and the players, both friends and foe, as he possibly can. Whether it's diving to save, positioning for a cross or narrowing the angle, the "open – looking out" position is critical, and will be referred to throughout the chapter. *Illustration 175* depicts a crossed ball situation, just one example to show the value of the open – looking out position.

Here the goalkeeper has his eye on the ball but because he is standing in a square position facing the winger with the ball, he cannot see the attacker on the run towards the near post nor is he aware of the position of his own defender or the attacker in the far post area.

Illustration 176 shows that while the actual location of the goalkeeper hasn't changed at all from *illustration 175*, his body position has. He is now turned into the open – looking out position where, at a glance, he can see the ball, the rest of the penalty area and the important players. These are all critical factors that will affect his decision when the cross is played in.

The goalkeeper must, in all situations, try to see as much of the field

175

of play, the players and the ball as possible. His view should never be obstructed unless circumstances are beyond his control. Look at the goalkeeper in *illustration 177 and 178* diving for the ball – even here the open – looking out position is adopted so that the keeper's own arms don't obstruct his view.

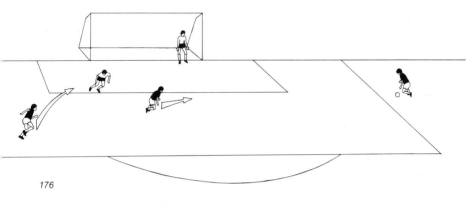

176

177

178

3. On the alert

Goalkeeping is as much a state of mind as a body position. Ready for action means that the keeper is aware of everything that is going on. *Concentration* is essential and needs to be worked on, as a keeper may be out of action for long periods. A player must *stay involved* by moving around, adjusting positions to every motion of the ball, and talking to his own team mates – "Watch the winger, Fred", "Move out of defence, John" (see *illustration 204*).

Although a goalkeeper may not always be involved in the main action, he is *always* in the game and may be required to act at any second.

Into action

Moving into action has to be done skilfully. For example, rushing out to challenge an attacker coming through with the ball may be just the thing the attacker wants as he sidesteps and goes around the overly eager keeper. That does not mean that the goalkeeper will not have to move at top speed at times, but it will depend on the situation.

Moving across the goal

Moving across the goal while maintaining the open position can be done in two ways.

180   181   182

179

1. **Side steps:** (see *illustration 179*). This is the best method when small adjustments of position become necessary and there is time to make those adjustments before returning to the ready position.

2. **Cross-legged run:** Running quickly across the goal – to intercept a ball, or to make ground to then dive on or at the ball or to move from the near post to the far post on a crossed ball – necessitates a quicker method than side steps. As *illustrations 180 to 186* show, the cross-legged run maintains the open position reasonably well and will certainly enable a final flying dive to be performed, if necessary, in the sideways open position.

Straightforward running and sprinting across the goal is a last

183   184   185   186

resort, to be used only when desperately fast action is necessary as the open position is lost for that moment. There will be times, of course, when all that matters is getting across the goal as quickly as possible to save the day!

Moving out of goal

As an attacker runs with the ball towards the goal, the situation itself will dictate what the goalkeeper's most appropriate course of action should be. Perhaps he'll need to sprint out of goal, or move more slowly towards the attacker and gradually narrow the angle, or stay on his goal line and let his fellow defenders make the challenge. Circumstances may require a quick-slow, quick-slow, cat-and-mouse run out of goal. Whatever action is called for, when it's time to repel the attack and capture the ball, the goalkeeper had better be in the ready position – sometimes called the "set" position – and not still running forward as the ball, and maybe the attacking player, go past!

The gorilla

Back to the penalty box zoo analogy, only now, the keeper becomes a gorilla. The round-shouldered and on the toes position, should be maintained on the run out of goal. Any goalkeeper coming out too upright, or worse, reeling back on his heels at the moment of the shot (see *illustrations 187, 188 and 189*), will make things too easy for the opposing player. Recoiling back, as in *illustration 189*, makes it impossible for the keeper to dive forwards or sideways. In fact he is really in no position to defend his goal. Such a posture can also raise questions about the goalkeeper's bravery.

The gorilla run maintains the open position with the weight on the balls of the feet, and the head slightly in advance of the rest of the body. From this posture, the run can be quickly converted into the ready position. A goalkeeper must remain **as big as possible for as long as possible**. A gorilla is a frightening animal at any time, but just ask people whether they would prefer a gorilla standing in front of them, or one lying down. We all know the answer. Therefore, the keeper/gorilla shouldn't go down until the very last second, if at all.

Body behind the ball

Before going into the specifics of the action, it almost goes without saying that a goalkeeper should get as much of the body behind the ball

RIGHT

WRONG

WRONG

187

188

189

WRONG

RIGHT

190

191

as possible. It's amazing, though, how many youngsters ignore that simple principle.

Perhaps we should say *"as much of the body as you can possibly get behind the ball"*. "As much" may be only:

One finger tip
Or better – one hand;
Or better still – two hands;
Or two hands with the double insurance of the face or chest behind the hands;
Or – best of all – the whole of the body behind and wrapped around the ball.

As much of the body behind the ball as possible is the key.

I would much rather have a goalkeeper called "flashy" because he exaggerates the need to get as much of the body behind the ball as possible – even on simple, straightforward shots. The goalkeeper in *illustration 190* is a lazy gambler, and living dangerously. In *191*, however, he is taking no chances and is absolutely right.

So while "body behind the ball" is a simple request, the aspiring goalkeeper has to work hard to accomplish it. To assist in the "body behind the ball" principle, a goalkeeper needs to be:

1. Ready and on his toes – prepared for anything – not jumping up and down.
2. On the move towards the shot early and swiftly, in order to get as much of the body behind the ball as possible. It may only be a finger tip

192

193

because of the speed of the shot – better that than no finger at all. Or it may be the whole of the body, virtually guaranteeing no goal.

Now that we are "ready", we can move into **action** and know the requirements. Here comes the real test.

Action

In this segment, we will examine how a goalkeeper can best capture the ball, or at least divert it from the target (the back of the net).

Shot-stopping

If a goalkeeper is not very good at stopping shots at his goal, he should seriously question whether the position is for him or not. It's the obvious first requirement. But take heart – it can be learned. A misconception exists that goalkeepers are naturally agile. Not many are. However, agility can be acquired, and one of the best ways to develop it is to spend time practising shot-stopping!

A critical consideration in shot-stopping is the actual diving technique, whether that is down on the ground or a mid-air fling across the goal. The open – looking out position is still very much desired and forms the basis of the correct diving positions.

Side position

Look at *illustrations 192 and 193*. The side position is very much in keeping with the "open" consideration mentioned earlier. The side position has the following advantages:

1. It gives a view of the ball at all times, thus allowing some adjustment even with a deflected shot.
2. It gives a more comfortable landing position along the side of the body. The muscles of the shoulders, arms and thighs (see *illustration 195*), have a cushioning effect (compare that with the jarring, awkward position of the belly flopper in *illustration 194*).
3. It enables the keeper to put a smothering, protective shield around the ball without being overly concerned about the "crash landing" effect that would be experienced if falling awkwardly (see *illustration 195*).
4. When catching the ball in mid-air, the side position allows it to be brought into a "fully claimed", or at the very least, a partially protected position, before the actual landing.
5. It allows the player to recover quickly back onto the feet (see Recovery, page 188).

194

WRONG

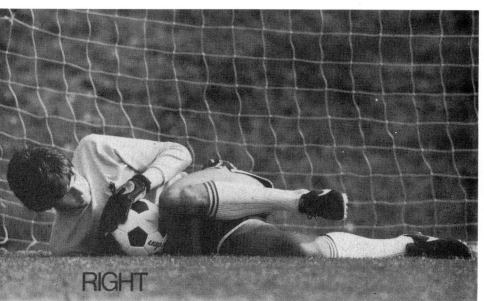

RIGHT

195

196

WRONG

WRONG

197

WRONG

198

It is very important that the side position be maintained after landing. *Illustration 196* shows what happens when a goalkeeper rolls onto his back after landing – the ball is exposed and therefore invites an attacker to dispute possession; or worse, the ball can flip out of the grasp when the keeper rolls onto his back. Another disadvantage is that the goalkeeper is in no position to recover quickly to start a counterattack.

Illustrations 197 and 198, on the other hand, show how the jarring fall of a front dive can shoot the ball from the grasp of the goalkeeper.

The side position is, without a doubt, the answer to most diving problems. The goalkeeper should maintain the side position on landing and so make sure the ball is fully claimed. A useful tip is to consciously draw the top knee in towards the stomach (see *illustration*

199), and at the same time turn the head and face into the upper knee (*illustration 200*). This action will maintain the side position and complete the smothering of the ball, but still enable the goalkeeper to quickly recover, once confident that everything is under control.

Narrowing the angle

Narrowing down the attacker's shooting angle is another vital aspect of goalkeeping that requires frequent and realistic practice. Coming off the goal line too early and too far will expose the goalkeeper to the chip shot. Also, showing too much of the near or far post will make it easier for the shooter. Consider the following salient points in angling:

199

200

201

202

203

1. Approach the shooter in the open/gorilla positions. Decide the speed of the movement out of goal. Sometimes it may have to be very fast to cut down the angle, other times more gradual. Whatever, the goalkeeper should be in a composed gorilla position *at the moment of the shot* – unless he has been required to dive at the feet of the incoming player.

2. Be wary about trying to anticipate a shot, having successfully narrowed the angle. Often, the goalkeeper will move too early and "sell" himself, making it easy for the shooter. In most cases, staying on your feet is the key, as this will keep the pressure on the shooter. From this position, the goalkeeper will react naturally when a shot is taken.

3. When compelled to move off the centre line out from the goal, a goalkeeper should make sure that the near post is adequately covered, even at the expense of the far post to some extent. The near post is the easiest, most inviting shot for the attacker. The far post is the furthermost shot, requiring much more accuracy, and there is always the chance that the shot could be cut out by a recovering defender even when the goalkeeper is beaten. Therefore, the shooter should be influenced by an "encouragement" to go for the far post by blocking out the near. *It must not be over-exaggerated. It's merely a question of degree (see illustrations 201 to 203).*

Stand up and be counted

Mention has already been made in this chapter about not lying down on the job. The dive is the last desperate effort to save a goal – brought about through necessity. No goalkeeper would *choose* to defend his goal by sitting or lying down. As a starting position, it would be laughable. But going down too early is almost as bad – it makes it so much easier for the opposition. So stay on your feet for as long as possible. It puts the pressure on the attacker. It's also a real test of character for the goalkeeper.

Through-balls

The judgment of the through-ball is probably the most difficult part of goalkeeping because the keeper must:

1. Judge the speed of the ball coming towards the goal.
2. Judge the positions of the attacker and recovering defenders.
3. Judge the speed of the oncoming players in relation to the ball and his own position in goal.

It is like travelling in a car and trying to guess the speed of another vehicle coming towards you. The goalkeeper – like the car driver who pulls out to pass a vehicle in front of him, with another coming towards him – must get it right the first time or there will be big trouble. The consequences of getting it wrong for the goalkeeper are not as serious as for the car driver – at worst, it's only a goal! But no goalkeeper wants to concede goals, so frequent through-ball practice is essential. This will improve a keeper's accuracy in judging distances and speed in relation to the positions of players.

One factor that will greatly help in dealing with through-balls is the starting position of the goalkeeper when the through-ball is played (see *illustration 204*). If play is in the other penalty area, the goalkeeper can afford to be on the edge of his own – preferably with his back defenders pushed up to or near the half-way line (remember the offside rule and how that can help in defending). Thus, if a very long clearance is hit towards the goal, the keeper can come out of his penalty area and kick it to safety, or he can retreat back towards his own goal in sufficient time to avoid exposure to the chipped shot.

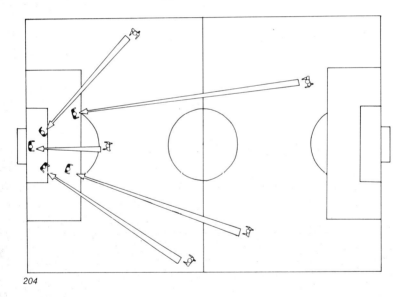

204

Illustration 204 shows what approximate "advanced" positions a goalkeeper can afford to take off his goal line in order to improve his dealings with a through-ball or a long clearance – always with enough to retreat to his own goal line if need be. So, the goakeeper should be moving forwards and backwards as the play ebbs and flows. It keeps him involved and alert, and very much assists his positional play. What's more, he becomes a full participating member of the team unit.

Diving at feet

Goalkeepers have a reputation for being fearless, mainly due to their readiness to dive at forwards' feet. Learned properly and practised correctly, diving at the feet does not require excessive courage, but it *does* require good timing, judgment and technique.

Normally, diving at the feet becomes necessary only when an attacker decides to dribble past the goalkeeper. Nearly all the factors previously mentioned – the open/gorilla position, staying on the feet – come into effect as the goalkeeper initially advances towards the attacker. The keeper must not commit himself to diving too early, though, or he will help the attacker make up his mind. The attacker could elect to take avoiding action and so dribble more easily around the fallen keeper.

The final, well-timed act of diving at the attacker's feet should be done initially in the open position, hands and arms in advance and ready for the ball – this will protect the head from being kicked (see *illustration 205*). Spreading the body sideways in the open position gives the least scoring opportunity to the attacking player.

Illustrations 205, 206 and 207 provide graphic examples of good and bad diving technique. Look at the photographs. Going in headfirst as in

205

206

207

208

209

210

illustration 207 is reckless, foolhardy, and worse – poor goalkeeping. The keeper is not presenting the biggest possible obstacle to the attacker, as is being achieved in *illustration 206*. The same is true of the feet-first effort in *illustration 209*. In *illustration 208*, the feet should be towards the centre of the goal, with the head pointing towards the outside – *not* the other way, as is shown here. Even in last-ditch circumstances, the principle of shutting out the near post as much as possible is at work. See how the upper body and arms cover the near post more efficiently than the feet in *illustration 210*. Besides, much more of the goal is covered by the keeper in *illustration 210* than in *208* – and should a shot be played across the goalkeeper towards the far post, it will very likely hit or be struck by the legs.

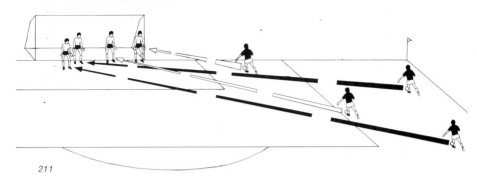

211

212

WRONG

213

RIGHT

Having gathered the ball, the goalkeeper *should not* be tempted to roll over and present his back to the attacker for three sound reasons:

1. As the goalkeeper rolls over, the ball may spin out of his hands.
2. The back of the head and the body are exposed and could be kicked.
3. The open position will have been sacrificed, and recovery for the counter-attack forfeited.

Crossed balls

I said earlier that through-balls are the most difficult, but crossed balls present goalkeepers with the greatest *number* of difficulties. I am not contradicting myself. There are many more crossed balls than through-balls – an average of 10 to one.

When a goalkeeper leaves his line to deal with a cross, he must make a solid contact with the ball or he has failed. This puts tremendous pressure on the keeper.

As indicated earlier in this chapter, the initial position of the goalkeeper is of utmost importance.

The open – looking out position ensures that the goalkeeper has a clear view of the ball, the penalty area and the players within it. But while the open – looking out/ready posture should not vary, the actual position of the goalkeeper will – depending on where the cross is coming from (see *illustration 211*).

Under normal circumstances, the goalkeeper should not stand waiting for a cross to arrive, since he can easily be knocked out of the challenge, as is shown in *illustration 212*. Ideally, he ought to be moving as he catches the ball, not only to give momentum to the leap, should one be required, but to help counter the physical challenge (see *illustration 213*).

However, there are times when a cross drops right underneath the crossbar, with the goalkeeper caught waiting for it. Even in such a situation, it is recommended that half a pace backwards be taken *if possible* so that the goalkeeper can move forward half a yard to attack the cross. If that can't be done, the goalkeeper must be resolute, take the ball and the knocks, and hope for – but not count on – the support of the referee if unfairly challenged.

Catching and punching

A frequently asked question is, "When should a goalkeeper catch the ball and when should he punch?" Simply stated, he should attempt to catch the ball whenever possible because of the real risks involved in

RIGHT

214

RIGHT

215

216 Two fists are better than one

punching. No matter how good the punch is, it is almost impossible to determine which player the ball will go to – friend or foe. If foe, then a first-time shot could well catch the goalkeeper in a poor defending position, having come off his goal line to punch the ball. Remember, too, that a punch will seldom travel very far from goal.

So the goalkeeper should risk punching only on those occasions when trying to catch the ball is even riskier. He should consider punching only when:

1. Under heavy challenge, his arms could easily be obstructed, possibly causing a dropped ball (see *illustration 214*).
2. He must go through and reach over players to make contact with the ball. In such a situation, mis-handling becomes a high risk (see *illustration 215*).
3. He has come out for a cross but finds that the ball is further out and a little higher than he had first anticipated. Here, a two-handed catch, if attempted, could result in a dropped ball.

In the last case, we are probably talking about a one-handed punch because the goalkeeper is over-reaching. However, our earlier principle, "as much of the body behind the ball as possible", applies to punching as well. Therefore, a two-handed punch gives a greater contact area than a one-handed, and reduces the chances of a mis-punch (see *illustration 216*).

Capturing the ball

The final action of claiming the ball is all part of the total task of goalkeeping. The goalkeeper should put such a tight hold on the ball that the enemy is totally discouraged from disputing possession. The objective should be to "melt" the ball into the goalkeeper's body as he receives it. So once more, it's back to the zoo!

The octopus action

As the goalkeeper receives the ball, he should absorb it into the body like an octopus. An octopus sucks in everything as it claims its victims; in goalkeeping, the "victim" is the ball. On making contact, the "drawing in" process begins, and continues until the ball disappears from sight – at which point the ambitions of the opposing forwards are comletely frustrated.

The octopus action has other advantages. As with ball control for an outfield player, where the pace of the ball is absorbed by the cushion-

217   218   219   220

ing effect of withdrawing the controlling surface, the melting-in effect (see *illustrations 217 to 220*) can help take the pace off the shot, and minimise the chances of the ball bouncing out of the hands. The drawing-in and wrapping-around process should be observed, whether it's a higher shot, a cross, or a ground shot requiring a diving save.

Recovery

Let us now turn our attention to another vital aspect of goalkeeping – **recovery**. Recovery applies in two distinctly different ways:

1. Where a goalkeeper has dived to the ground and successfully claimed the ball, with the requirement then to quickly launch a counter-attack and so catch the opposition off-balance.
2. After a goalkeeper has committed himself to a dive or moved out of his goal for a cross or a through-ball, but for a combination of reasons, has not claimed the ball. The ball remains in the danger area, and the goalkeeper must recover it as quickly as possible into a good position to once again defend the goal.

There are two main types of recovery:

221

222

223
224

1. Recovery from the ground

If a goalkeeper has gone to ground for whatever reason – a dive, or to block a shot – the objective, if he hasn't got the ball, is to recover back on to the feet as quickly as possible. Even when the ball is claimed, the keeper should think in terms of a quick recovery so as to start a counter-attack. That is why once again, the side position along with the open – looking out consideration offer so many advantages. *Illustrations 221 to 224* show the jack-in-the-box effect of the recovery from the side position which can be achieved with practice. It is done by a roll-up, a push from the hands, and a final, thrust-from-the-legs type action.

2. Recovery back to goal

Being caught out of goal with the ball still in play causes a dilemma. Do you stand your ground and defend from where you are, or do you sprint back to the goal line? It will all depend on the situation. If an opponent has the ball and is about to shoot, there may be no choice but to stand your ground or else do something desperate, such as diving at the feet of the player to block the shot. However, if there is time, and the ball is out of the immediate danger area and not likely to be struck at once, chances are the best action is to get back to the goal line – or thereabouts – as fast as your legs will carry you. *Just one proviso:* if at all possible, a goalkeeper shouldn't turn his back on play and, in particular, the ball when sprinting back towards the goal – for all the reasons we have talked about in this chapter.

No goalkeeper is perfect and everyone will make mistakes. A quick recovery can rectify many. On the positive side, the greatest feats of goalkeeping have come from "double saves". Imagine this situation: the goalkeeper comes quickly off his line, and dives at the feet of an onrushing forward making a great block. The ball, however, rebounds to an opponent on the edge of the penalty area who chips a shot towards the unguarded goal. But our hero has made a jack-in-the-box recovery and while sprinting back towards the goal, launches himself upwards and backwards to turn the goal-bound shot over the bar. Fantastic? Yes and no. It happens, and is achieved by a combination of good basic goalkeeping. You don't have to be Superman to be a good goalkeeper!

We have the ball! – distribution

Frequently, the goalkeeper becomes the first attacker of his team. As soon as the ball is claimed by the keeper, he stops being a defender and immediately begins his attacking duties. The use of the ball – by kicking and throwing – is a vital part of the goalkeeping skill, and a keeper who is poor in this department weakens his team. The key, then, is to practise kicking and throwing regularly.

Kicking practice – off the ground with a conventional goal-kick, or out of the hands, with a punt or a dropped volley – can be undertaken either on your own or with your team, possibly under the supervision of the coach.

(One word of warning, however: be careful when practising the dropped volley kick. It is a highly skilled technique with a high risk factor if the ball is mis-kicked.)

If you are practising on your own, using several balls will spare you considerable jogging between kicks. Throwing practice will be dealt with in Part 2 of this chapter.

Summary

1. You need to be "ready" – on your toes, "looking out", alert and concentrating.
2. Retain the "open" position whenever possible in every facet of the goalkeeping function.
3. Stay on your feet for as long as you can.
4. Stay as big as possible for as long as you can – do a "gorilla" of a job!
5. Claim the ball like an octopus and suck it into the body and out of sight.
6. "Recover" with or without the ball as **quickly** as you can – to start an attack or to be ready to defend once again.

Part 1 of Goalkeeping has dealt with the fundamental considerations and how they are applied in the specific tasks of a goalkeeper.

Part 2 will provide the practices that will help a goalkeeper make significant improvements – and so allow a young player to either "manufacture" himself, or to be "manufactured" by the parent/coach.

The terrific thing about goalkeeping is that it's fun. My old maths teacher, after seeing me perform in goal, once commented, "The sooner Waiters realises that goalkeeping is a science and not a series of acrobatic leaps, the sooner he will become a really good goalkeeper". He was only half right. No matter how good one's positional play is, the final, acrobatic leaping effort will be the icing on the cake – the spectacular difference between a save and a goal. The goalkeeping science and the gymnastic performance can both be learned and practised.

PART 2

♨ SECTION I

The practices

There are dozens of goalkeeping practices that a young player can get involved in, both on his own and with his friends. It is important, however, for the goalkeeper either to analyse his own performance and decide what type of practice is most necessary, or to ask a parent or team coach for an assessment. Then a practice schedule can be devised, using this book, to help overcome those weaknesses.

This section will give you ideas for practice, but I would suggest that if you are enthusiastic about the goalkeeping position, you find the time to read carefully (and if necessary, read again) the principles and recommendations contained in Part 1 of this chapter. You will better understand your strong points and be able to identify those techniques that need extra work.

Practice 1a
The rebound surface

First find a rebound wall and if there is a soft surface (grass or sand) adjacent to it, so much the better.

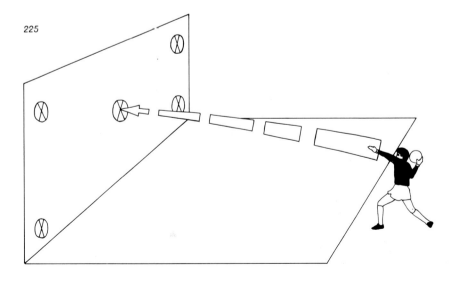

225

226

Mark targets on the wall as indicated in *illustration 225* with chalk or paint.

As well, mark a line 15 to 20 yards away. In this situation, practise your throwing. There are any number of different throwing techniques – use whichever techniques you are most comfortable with to hit one of the four targets. Keep track of the number of hits per throw taken, and try to top your record each practice. As you improve over a long period of time, move the throwing line four to five yards further back.

Practice 1b

Using the same rebound wall and adjacent soft surface, set up the practice shown in *illustation 226*. By kicking and throwing the ball against the wall, you can give yourself a variety of different saves to make. The way you throw or kick the ball will give you a fair idea of where it is likely to return, but this practice will still help you establish correct driving techniques.

Back in my professional days in Blackpool I was fortunate enough to have a sea-wall and soft sand as my rebound area. The sea-wall was made of irregularly shaped stones so the rebounds were unpredictable, realistic and challenging. The height of the sea-wall also allowed me to practise my goal-kicking without the problem of lengthy retrieval runs in between – but I practised only when the tide was out. Naturally!

227

Practice 2

If there are two of you, both with a liking for goalkeeping, set up two practice goals as shown in *illustration 227*. Make the goals eight yards wide and approximately 15 yards apart. Using a variety of shots such as thrown balls, kicks and punts, the two of you can practise a whole range of "stops". The secret is to try to "extend" one another rather than score every time, so that good, meaningful practice can be obtained without the frustration and disruption of always having to chase and retrieve balls.

Practice 3

This practice is for two players, one acting as the goalkeeper and the other as attacker. A decision is made as to the minimum distance from

228

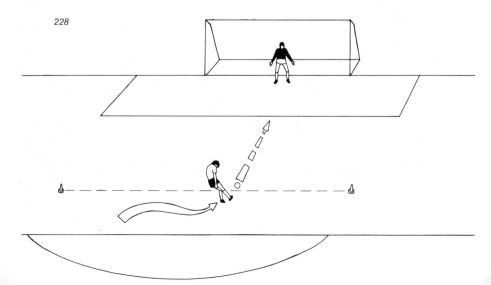

which the ball can be shot. In *illustration 228*, a line has been marked by cones halfway between the penalty spot and the penalty area. The attacking player can start from anywhere outside the agreed-upon line and must touch the ball at least once before shooting, as the shot can be taken only with a moving ball. The scoring is simple. One *goal* for an authentic goal, and one *goal* for the first-class save. And that's perhaps where the simplicity ends! Both of you must agree on what constitutes a first-class save. Try it, you'll like it. Even if you do argue a bit!

🌀 🌀 SECTION II

The practices in Section I can benefit enormously from the presence and help of the parent/coach, and are easily modified to accommodate the numbers and facilities you have available.

Practice 4
The six shot-stop

This is a practice in shot-stopping and recovery. You can play with one ball but two or more would be preferable. As *illustration 229* shows, the coach stands on the six-yard line and throws a shot at the goalkeeper. These can vary from high and low shots to rolled shots into the corners

229

and balls thrown down to both sides of the goalkeeper to simulate downward headers.

You want the goalkeeper extended but not beaten. With only one ball, the object should be to try to make the shot difficult but catchable and so keep the sequence going. The goalkeeper is required to return the ball from his hands as soon as he claims it. Having done so, he immediately recovers – jack-in-the-box style – to the ready position. This is not exactly the way it happens in an actual game, as a goalkeeper would hold the ball, recover quickly and then look to use it. But in this practice, our objectives are to improve players' diving techniques, reaction, agility and recovery.

To achieve those objectives, throwing the ball back quickly and accurately – even from a lying position – is necessary. It is followed immediately by a fast recovery, with the next shot on its way almost at the moment the ready position is resumed. This maintains the rapid sequence that is essential in the practice.

Don't be tempted to make it a 10-shot practice – this is not an endurance test. Fatigue will cause sloppy techniques and could lead to bad habits. Allow sufficient time after each six-shot stop for the goalkeeper to recover his composure so that he is raring-to-go again.

Practice 5
Cross and throw

The challenging role of the goalkeeper is best demonstrated by the cross-catch-throw sequence. The goalkeeper begins by defending his goal against the cross but once he claims the ball, he is an attacker. A quick and accurate throw often results in a very telling attack on the other goal – particularly since the opposition is usually caught "on the wrong foot" as its members have moved in to attack the goal from the cross. It seems that the goalkeeper almost takes a Jekyll and Hyde personality. The determined, no-nonsense, defending goalkeeper who

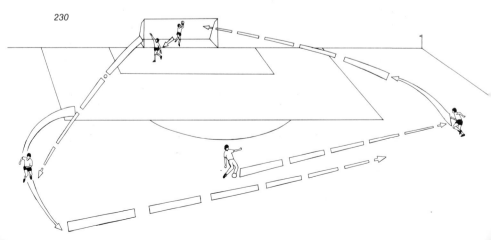

230

has aggressively challenged to catch the cross must now change into a composed and skilful throwing attacker. Just watch a top quarterback in American football for the composure he brings to his throwing, even when under considerable pressure. *Illustration 230* shows a combined practice including the cross-throw situation.

The minimum requirement is three players, so if there are only two, Dad pitches in and becomes the third. The winger receives a service from the coach, runs and crosses the ball into the goal area. The goalkeeper fields the cross and immediately "switches play" with a throw to the feet of the defender. The defender controls the ball and moves 10 yards forward, and then hits a long cross-field ball back to the winger who starts the sequence again. If the distance from the defender to the winger is too great – very young players would find it impossible – the ball should be relayed back across the field from the defender to the coach. The coach would then start the sequence all over again.

Alternatively, the defender can move towards the centre of the penalty area and pass the ball out to the winger, then hold his position in the penalty area, as shown in the illustration, until the goalkeeper catches the cross and then he can break out wide for the throw. In a game, the defender – if he were a defender or midfielder – would actually come into the penalty area to support his team in defending against the cross and then break out once the goalkeeper had safely gathered the ball, taking up a receiving attacking position as shown in the illustration. Players should change positions regularly and so receive practice in all three roles.

Practice 6
The back flip

Goalkeepers are compelled to come "off their line" to cut down the shooting angle, but as a result are sometimes caught "out" by a clever chipped shot or a high looping ball spinning up and out of a blocked challenge – or simply by a goalkeeper who makes a mis-judgement by coming out too far. Having to recover backwards to catch the ball, or push the ball over the bar, is extremely difficult but it occurs often enough in games to still warrant regular practice. *Illustration 231* shows why it is so difficult. As the goalkeeper recovers backwards, it is awkward for him to leap from this position as he tends to have his body weight and balance on his heels. Also, the angle of his body as he recovers back towards the goal can trick him into thinking he can make a stronger contact with the ball than he really can. The result is that the ball is merely being helped on its way into the net.

231

If the goalkeeper cannot safely catch the ball, the secret is for him to work hard to push the ball upwards – not backwards – and allow the momentum of the shot to take the ball back over and beyond the bar. You'll see in the illustration that the push of the ball is generally done with the open hand.

The practice is quite simple. The coach is positioned on the penalty spot. He lobs the ball by a foot volley or by hand over the head of the goalkeeper positioned towards the edge of the six-yard area who moves back for the recovery save (see *illustration 232*).

The goalkeeper must face up to the coach at the start of each service as if he were dealing with a straightforward shot, and therefore must not anticipate by half-turning. If the goalkeeper does anticipate, he should be punished by the coach shooting on his blind side as he turns away. This type of save requires great effort by the goalkeeper, who should be given sufficient time between each shot to recover his composure.

Summary

Flip back to the practices in the Shooting and Crossing and Heading chapters for other ideas – in particular, those that give "combined practice" opportunities, allowing different skills to be worked on at the same time. Combined practices that involve strikers, defenders, and players attacking from wing positions are excellent. They add realism and give the extra dimension of a game situation.

232

🔵🔵🔵 SECTION III

Introduction

One major difficulty for the coach is that he cannot plan the team session just for the benefit of the goalkeepers. (With younger players, it does not present the same problems. They should not have permanent positions – only inclinations – and must practise regularly in all positions.) In a team situation, however, goalkeepers inevitably "emerge". They have to be selected for the games, and too often they are chosen solely because of their size. So goalkeeping becomes "their position". It is impossible to provide a hard and fast answer to the problem except to say that it is wrong to "condemn" a player to one position too early in his soccer development. Nevertheless, the coach must address the needs of the goalkeeping function in one way or another. Combined practices, such as those outlined below, are ideal as they allow shooting, crossing, defending, and other skills to be practised as the same time as goalkeeping.

Still, there will be times when the team session just does not lend itself to the needs of the goalkeeper. In these cases, don't be afraid to send two or three goalkeepers off on their own to another part of the training area – particularly if you have already shown them practices such as 2, 3, 4 and 6, or have reviewed kicking and throwing practices with them. Help them get organised while the rest of the group is enjoying a fun-drill, and then leave them alone. Goalkeepers will normally practise very well with a minimum of supervision.

Sending goalkeepers off on their own almost contradicts what I have said earlier about not condemning them to one position or ostracising them from the team. Great care must be exercised here. Try to establish the right mix – specific practice with team integration. So a further personal plea from an ex-goalkeeper is to spend an extra 10 or 15 minutes at the end of the team session with those players who are inclined towards the goalkeeping position, particularly when goalkeeping has not been adequately covered in the main practice. The goalkeeper will really appreciate it and your effort will be well rewarded by their response. Believe me!

The goalkeeping consideration has no set rules. Goalkeepers must be an integral part of the team but do require specific attention. As the coach, you are the cook and must decide what proportions go into the "mix". I hope my suggestions help with the recipe.

Practice 7

This practice (see *illustration 233*) is essentially the same as Practice 7, of Chapter 3, Shooting for Goal. Refer back to page 72 of that chapter to see how this practice is organised. The objective here though, is to improve goalkeeping in the narrowing of the angle. As part of a team session, this exercise fits in very well as a combined skills practice. The coach's skill can make it enjoyable and purposeful for all players. But

233

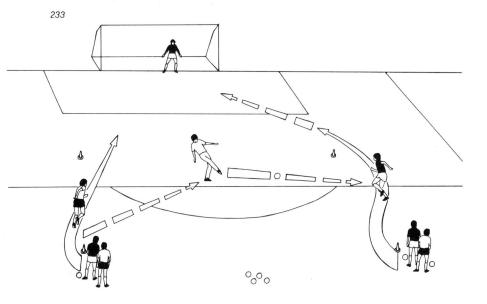

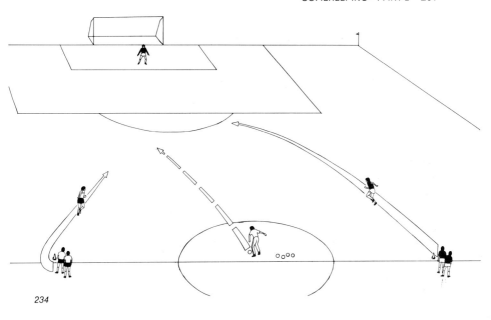

234

he'll have to keep one careful eye on the goalkeepers. With more than one goalkeeper, each can take a shift – facing, say, six shots a turn. Consider having another person act as the coach/server so that you are free to observe more clinically the actions and reactions of the goal-keepers.

The practice can be made competitive by setting up two teams, each with a goalkeeper. One team is "on", the other is "off" behind the goal retrieving the balls. The team off the field has its nominated goalkeeper in goal. Each team takes 20 shots; the winning team is the one scoring the most goals.

Practice 8
Through-ball

The coach, with a supply of balls, is situated on the half-way line in the centre circle. Two files of players line up at the marker cones (see *illustration 234*). Younger players could start from cones nearer to the goal. The coach plays the ball forward, biasing the service either left or right. The first man to reach the ball becomes the attacker, with the second player becoming the recovering defender. Thus the practice is a one versus one with a goalkeeper. The coach should also serve some balls that are 50/50 in terms of the goalkeeper and the leading player from the cones. In this situation, the goalkeeper must decide either to come out and collect the ball (or even kick it if out of his penalty area) or to hold his position and then advance to narrow the angle.

Practice 9

This practice offers an excellent workout in shooting even though the purpose here is to concentrate on goalkeeping. The coach, situated centrally just inside the penalty area, serves by hand a variety of balls to the players situated at the cones – one ball and one player at a time! Balls are rolled, bounced and lobbed in the air in any number of ways to simulate the different types of circumstances and shots that occur in a game. The goalkeeper needs to read the type of shot that is likely to come in. For instance, with a quick, rolled ball he can afford to come off his line two or three yards to cut down the shooting angle. With a bounced or lobbed ball, however, he must be wary of a dipping volley and so position himself on or near his line. The starting position of the shooters is moved periodically to each of the three cones.

Once again, the team group can be split into two – one shooting, one fielding – for purposes of competition. Because of the varied service desired, the coach will no doubt be accused of having favoured the winning group with easier service. The coach can never win! But of course, one team will – in spite of the complaints. To add additional realism to the practice, position an assistant lurking outside the six-yard box, to pick up any rebounds, should the goalkeeper not handle clearly.

Summary

This is one of the heftier chapters in the book, and yet there is so much more that can be said about the intricacies of goalkeeping.

I urge you to review other relevant chapters – on crossing, heading, shooting – for further practices that incorporate crucial aspects of the goalkeeping role. Give your goalkeepers the help and support they deserve, work conscientiously on the practices – especially the "combined" practices – outlined here, and your players are sure to improve and do their coach proud.

Chapter 10
GOING FORWARD TOGETHER - ATTACKING SUPPORT

🏐 SECTION I

How can one player without the ball help another with the ball to pass it? The answer is simple – by moving into a position which makes it easier for the player with the ball to make his pass.

The basic attacking unit is three. Whether it's 11-a-side or a scaled-down version such as five-a-side, the game is played in units of three, and then in triangles. I will explain how that works later. For the moment, just remember that the combination of three will provide the basis for almost all attacking tactics in soccer.

Every player within passing distance of another player who has possession of the ball should be thinking, "How can I help my team mate? How can I give him additional alternatives? What position can I take up that will help him and help the team?"

235

1. Passing angles

A player should not position himself where he cannot receive the ball if he wants to make himself available for a pass to help a nearby team mate in possession.

In *illustration 235*, the player with the ball is going to find it extremely difficult to pass to his team mate without risking an interception. But if the player "off-the-ball" moves in either of the directions indicated, he opens up an angle that will help his team mate pass to him relatively easily.

2. Square passes – beware!

I was always taught in my early soccer days that, "If you *can*, pass forward; if you *can't*, pass backwards. If you can't do either, be careful!" What are termed "square passes" – balls played sideways (see *illustration 236*) – are easily anticipated and intercepted. When this happens, at least two attackers – possibly more – are caught out of position, on the "wrong side of the ball". Meanwhile, their team is put on the defensive because of the bad pass and the poor supporting positions, and what is more, the team is forced to defend without the two "culprits" who lost possession. So if square passes are extremely risky, support-

236

ing players should not take up positions that encourage a square ball.

In *illustration 237*, the strong supporting positions of players 2 and 3 have given player 1 three alternatives:

1. Take on the defender 4 while player 5 is "occupied" by 2 and so not in a good covering position.
2. Pass the ball inside to 2 who has earned himself space to receive the pass and given 1 a good passing angle. However, the pass will have to be accurate, or 5 could intercept.
3. Play the ball back to 3 and so keep possession of it without risking its loss.

Notice that the supporting positions of 2 and 3 give a triangular shape to the basic unit of three. The shape of the triangle will, of course, change but a *triangle* of one kind or another formed by lines connecting the players should always be there.

237

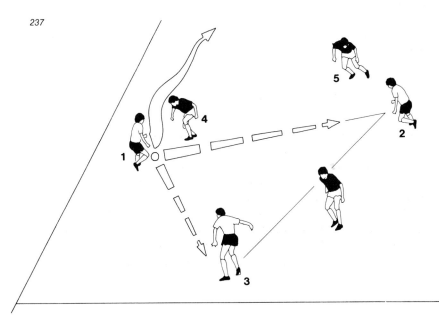

3. *Unselfish running*

A player's unselfish running into a position that will occupy a defender and take him out of a good defending position is not only praiseworthy but skilful. Unfortunately, it is not always appreciated by team mates, coaches or onlookers.

In *illustration 238*, player 2 has run across the field taking with him the defender, and moved into the area of the other defender. By his unselfish action, 2 has occupied two defenders, and created a big chunk of space for player 3 to receive a pass from 1. This is an example of the exception to the rule of always trying to make oneself available for the pass. In this case, unselfish running and occupying defenders have made things easier for both the player with the ball and the player receiving the ball.

4. *Don't all go away, but don't all come to the ball!*

A very common sight with young players involved in an 11-a-side situation is to see most of the 22 participants gathered around the ball, all

238

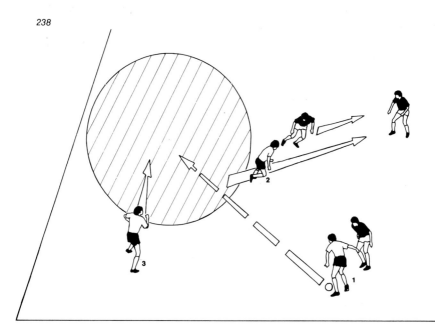

239

trying to get a kick. It is one very good reason for mini-soccer (a scaled-down version of the game in five- and six-a-side) which guarantees, by the law of averages, that each player will get more kicks of the ball than in 11-a-side play because there are fewer players kicking one ball. Whether it's five-a-side or 11-a-side, all the players should not gather around the ball. On the other hand, if everyone runs away from the player with the ball, that makes the passing player's task impossible, too. So a combination of the two is necessary.

As you can see in *illustration 239*, the passing angles are fine and so is the triangular shape that gives support to the man on the ball. But

240

RIGHT

241

players 2 and 3 have moved in too close to the ball and the defenders have been pulled in with them as well – only making it tighter for the attackers and consolidating the defenders' own positions. Any pass will give the defenders a chance to challenge for the ball.

Illustration 240 shows the "going away" extreme. As 3 and 2 disappear into the distance, 1 is left in an isolated one versus one situation against the defender.

It could be argued that in certain circumstances – and particularly if player 1 is a very good dribbler – the ploy is perfectly fine. But in truth, the lack of a real passing alternative reduces 1's options and thus he cannot fake to pass or dribble quite as convincingly. Less confused, the defender knows his only task is to stop 1 from dribbling past.

Illustration 241 shows player 3 taking away the covering defender while 2 moves in to give closer support to the player on the ball. Player 3 can always check back into the space he has created to receive a pass. Attacker 2 has moved into a position which allows for a simple pass or even a quick "give and go" – thus creating all kinds of doubts in the mind of defender 4. He is unsure what 1 will do because of the number of alternatives.

Thus, a combination of *going away to take defenders away and going towards the player with the ball to give passing alternatives* is what you want to strive for. This consideration of room in which to play will be covered more specifically in Chapter 12, The Creation of Space.

5. Removing the cover

Defenders in good covering positions – consider player 3 in *illustration 242* – make life difficult for a player such as 1 by seriously reducing his alternatives.

Player 3 is not only covering fellow defender 4, but is in a good marking position in relation to 2. But attacker 2 can move off in four directions, each of which will give the defender a real headache. The arrows indicate that the attacker can move forwards, sideways or backwards, leaving the defender with a major decision – should he go with the player or should he stay?

If he stays, 2 could well end up receiving the ball unmarked. If he goes with 2, he leaves defender 4 uncovered. By his actions, player 2 has done his team mate a good turn in upsetting and confusing the covering player, and he may have put himself in a better attacking position than his original position. Defenders are at their most composed when they can *see the ball and the opposition*, **and have both the ball and the opposition in front of them**. When the ball is played in behind defenders, they are on the wrong side of the ball and must work hard to get right side again.

Similarly, when an attacker is trying to get in behind defenders, defenders inevitably get anxious. "Blind side runs" or "threatening the backs of defenders" means making runs which force a defender to turn and look back, and so lose sight of the ball or, if he keeps watching the ball, lose sight of the man. Neither situation is a happy one for the defender. No matter what he does, he is wrong. He can't win.

242

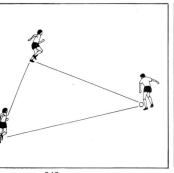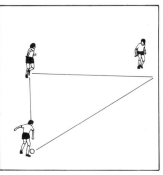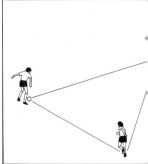

243

6. The triangle

Mention has already been made of the "triangle", as well as a cautious word injected about square passes. Just as three attacking players together form the true attacking unit, so the triangular consideration needs to be applied when three players are combining together.

The triangular arrangement of three players – no matter how it is changed around – ensures good support of the player on the ball and provides the angles for passing (see *illustration 243*).

Just one word of warning. Be careful of situations such as further developed in *illustration 244*. In any game, whether it be a three-a-side, a six-a-side or an 11-a-side, the back man – the very last man on the field (not including the goalkeeper) – should not be the one with the ball, for obvious reasons. If he loses the ball, there is no cover to prevent a strike at goal. But if, as in *illustration 244*, a triangular unit of three is combin-

244

ing together with other covering defenders *behind* the player on the ball, that is a different story. In these circumstances, he is not the last man with the ball anyway.

7. Communication

In these days of spare-part surgery, every soccer player's Christmas shopping list should include a request for a second pair of eyes, to be worn exclusively at the back of the head! Though that is probably not – realistically – for this century, the ability for a soccer player to see in every direction would be a wonderful advantage. Without that facility, team mates have to act as the extra pair of eyes – by means of communication. What's the point of being in an admirable position if your team mate doesn't know you are there? There are three main ways of communicating in soccer:

1. **Talking:** Short, sharp instructions are the order of the game. If you are long-winded, it will be too late.
2. **Signals:** A finger pointing here, a nod of the head there, a gesture with the arm – all will aid soccer communication.
3. **Eye contact:** Seeing "eye to eye" is essential for team spirit. But looking one another "in the eye" will help develop the right understanding to pick up all the little cues, including minor signals that can bamboozle the opposition.

Because three players form the basic attacking unit, seize any opportunity to play three-a-side. It is probably the finest practice game situation in which to learn *attacking approach play*.

This chapter and the following two do not contain practices for a youngster on his own. You cannot have a "team of one", and as all three chapters deal with basic team understanding, a minimum of three players is needed – a two versus one gives a "team" situation. (A team is any number of people combining together to form an effective unit.) So team play in soccer means anything from two players to 11.

Practice 1

Two versus one and three versus one. A two versus one situation as shown in *illustration 245* provides an excellent way to practise co-operation – in particular, the making of good angles which will enable the man with the ball to pass safely. Ball control and short passing are also incorporated, so this becomes a first-class combined skills practice. *Illustration 246* shows a similar situation but this time in a three versus one using a bigger area, thus allowing four players to become

245

246

involved and making it a little easier for the passing players. If the three players are finding it relatively easy against the one, make it two-touch or three-touch.

To make the practice a competition, introduce the following factors:

1. Each person has a turn as the defender.
2. The defender defends for three tries by the attackers.
3. The defender's objective is to keep consecutive passes to a minimum by intercepting, tackling, or forcing the error with the ball being played out of the area.
4. The winner is the defender with the lowest consecutive passes against total.

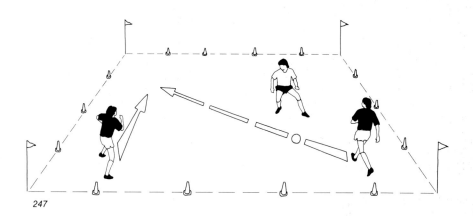

247

Practice 2

This progresses Practice 1 into more of a match situation. Use a 15-yard square, with a goal two yards wide set up 15 yards from the square, as shown in *illustration 247*. The two attackers start on the back line, one in possession of the ball. The defender must start in the middle of the square. The practice begins when either of the attackers moves from the line. The object is to get a shot on goal, but no one is allowed to leave the square. It gives the two against one situation a direction and purpose. Two attackers may keep possession until they make a real opening for a shot on goal. Bear in mind, however, that the more passes taken before a shot on goal, the greater the likelihood of a mis-placed pass, a tackle, or an interception made by the defender. **So players must think positive and go for goal.**

In competition, allow 10 tries per pair. The winner is the player with the best combined pairs goals total. The goals scored by the pair count for both players, and are added to the second pair total.

Practice 3
Two versus two or three versus three

As *illustration 248* indicates, the goals are five feet wide. Kick-ins are taken rather than throw-ins because of the small size of the field. Other-wise the rules – apart from no offside and no handling for goalkeepers – are the same as for the 11-a-side game.

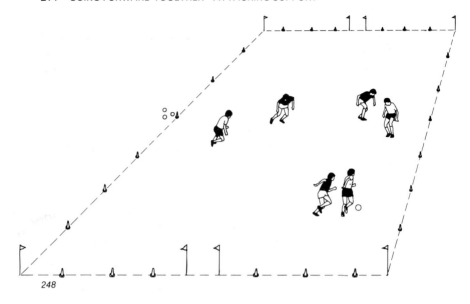

248

Summary

Playing a small-sided game such as three versus three is a terrific way to learn about soccer. When working four, five or six players, never hesitate to organise a game such as the one in Practice 3. It is no coincidence that the world's great soccer players spent considerable practice time in their younger days playing small-sided soccer games.

Once again, however, there has to be a note of caution. If all of a young player's practice time is spent on exercises such as Practice 3, he could end up a "short-game player". By that, I mean a player who deals mainly with five- and 10-yard passes, and who is reluctant to play the longer passes. Such a player might never learn how to cross a ball properly, for example. So small-sided games are excellent, but they are not the total answer.

🏐🏐 SECTION II

Part A – Two versus one or three versus one

This is exactly the same practice as Practice 1, but I make no apologies for that. The two versus one, three versus one practice can be really good fun. If there are only two or three young players, it gives the coach an opportunity to join in, and that adds a special dimension. Make it a rule, at least at the beginning, that the player who makes the mistake that spoils the sequence of consecutive passes becomes the defender. The coach will have to adjudicate in the event of a dispute – and you can guarantee there will be plenty. The best part, for the young players at least, is when the coach makes the mistake and ends up in the middle. The coach can employ some child psychology to keep the spirits running high, and the tempo lively. Even a little bit of playful "cheating" may be in order.

If the coach has joined in but there are three youngsters or more, he should periodically take himself out of the practice to observe and *instruct*. In a two versus one, or three versus one situation, several points will become very obvious and can and should be brought out:

1. Players need to move into a space to receive a pass.
2. If they are running around at breakneck speed, it will be very difficult to judge a pass for the receiving player and similarly difficult for the fast-moving player to control the ball or even himself! Sharpness and speed over five to six yards should not be confused with players who run around like scalded cats.
3. The players off-the-ball need to talk to the player on-the-ball – "hold it"; "give it to me"; "play it here" – making use, at the same time, of signals to help the player on-the-ball.
4. Players should utilise every inch of space available to them.

Part B - two versus two

As with Practice 3 (*illustration 248*), set up the game and let them play. Insist however, that *some* time be devoted to two-touch (see Conditioned Games, in Coaches' Segment). Not only will it help their passing and control but **they will be forced to take up good supporting positions or they will lose the ball**. As the coach, either involved in the game or supervising on the sidelines, you can have a major influence on the enthusiasm of the practice. Two versus two and three versus three situations are exhausting exercise if performed properly, so don't be afraid of having time-outs. The important factor is for youngsters to give their all when the ball is in play. With that in mind, try not to have too many unnatural breaks – those annoying delays when balls are kicked out of the practice area and everyone stands around waiting for one player to retrieve them. It is so much more convenient to have three or four balls on the sidelines and utilise them all. This will help keep the practice momentum running high.

Here's a valuable tip for two versus two play. Often, when left to their own devices, each pair of players will tend to play in "channels" – one on the left and one on the right. Subconsciously they will think, "this is

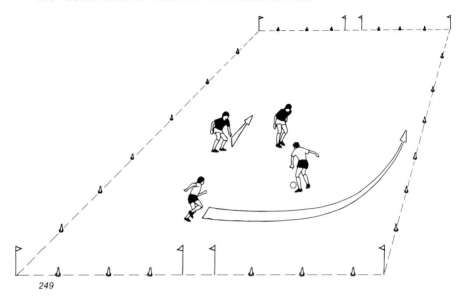

249

my side, I'd better stick to it''. To give defenders real problems as well as to open up the passing angles, encourage players to think of cross-over play as shown in *illustration 249*. Any type of cross-over or change in one's play can easily bamboozle the defenders – who marks who? – and open up more alternatives for the player with the ball.

SECTION III
Use the grid principle

Any number of team practice sessions can be organised using the grid principle (see Coaches' Segment, page 271). Use markers, existing lines, practice bibs, corner posts, or what have you to produce a number of 10 yard × 10 yard squares. *Illustration 250* shows how one versus one, two versus one, three versus one, four versus two's, two versus two's and three versus three's can all be accommodated using this principle. Only minor adjustments become necessary when moving from one practice to another.

Three-a-side tournament

When I first joined Liverpool F.C. as an assistant coach in the early 1970s, I spent many hours with Manager/Coach Bill Shankly, discussing what he expected from me with regard to the Youth Development

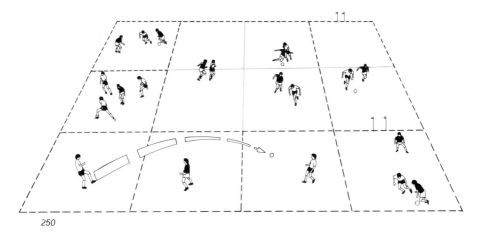

250

Programme for which I was responsible. "Shanks" told me of his early days at Liverpool, and how he organised many three-a-side sessions, selecting each team very carefully. He would choose the trios according to their proximity in the team – right back, centre back, right midfield would be one team; the two central strikers and a winger, another; and so on. He made sure that those players who combined together on a regular basis within the 11-man team also had the chance to do so in practice.

Apart from the togetherness aspect, it truly reinforced my belief in the three-a-side game. What was good enough for Bill Shankly and the first team players of Liverpool was good enough for me and the youth players – so I immediately instituted a weekly three-a-side tournament session for the young professionals. It wasn't too long before "Shanks" invited me to expand the tournament to take in the senior players. So I was designated "organiser", and with a senior and youth squad or over 30 players, it was a many-teamed affair.

I believe in the benefits of three-a-side play so strongly that I have no hesitation in recommending it as an important part of player development at any age and level of ability.

The following is a tournament format which you can use at a team practice session.

Three-a-side rules

1. No goalkeepers, no handling.
2. No throw-ins – use kick-ins, normal goal-kicks and corners.
3. Score from anywhere.
4. Goals two yards wide, approximately 4 to 5 feet high – depending on what is available, e.g., corner flags, etc.

Numbers organisation

Coping with unknown numbers arriving at the team practice requires improvisation and number juggling. The number-juggling table below shows the alternatives that can be used to ensure a fair tournament. With awkward numbers, a four-a-side format may have to be used.

Number juggling for three-a-side (four-a-side tournament)

15 No problem: 5×3
16 4-a-side (4 teams)
17 6 teams (coach joins in): 6×3
18 No problem: 6×3
19 4 teams of 4, one of 3; One team resting/refereeing: 3 teams supplemented by resting team or coach
20 5 teams of 4 or 6 teams of 3 and one of 2 using same principle as with 19
21 7 teams of 3, one resting
22 The awkward number: 6 teams of 3, one team of 4; coach always plays against 4
23 7 teams of 3, one team of 2, plus coach, or use 22 principle (minus coach)
24 No problem: 6×4 or 8×3

Any problem can be accounted for – with a little planning.

Example of tournament using five teams

Each team is assigned a name, although in this example, we are merely using A, B, C, D, and E.
Round one A versus B, C versus B, E spare – the referees!
Round two A versus C, D versus E, B – referees
Round three A versus D, D versus B, C – referees
Round four A versus E, B versus C, D – referees
Round five B versus D, C versus E, A – referees.

Five games lasting 10 minutes each will provide 50 minutes of play. With change-overs, the tournament should last approximately 70 minutes.

Organisational details

1. A playing captain is appointed for each team. He sometimes acts as the referee and judge – if there are no spare players or teams. He also acts as the "runner" and after each game, reports the score to the organiser. Captains of both teams report to the organiser to make sure that the score-line is authentic.

2. Each field is approximately 30 × 20 yards.

3. Each game lasts 10 minutes (or whatever time is agreed upon) with no half-time – in normal circumstances.

4. All games are started by the organiser's whistle and finish *immediately* on the final whistle.

5. Identification bibs are essential. Two sets (three or four) on each playing area. Bibs stay on the site as players change areas.

6. The final table is based on two points for a win, one point for a tie. Teams on level points are separated by a goal difference, and if no tie-breaker, by most goals scored.

7. If a play-off is desired, then the same formula as (6) is used for "seeding" in play-off formula.

Too often, coaches look for the answer to team understanding by playing 11-a-side soccer or by informing players that, "You're a right back – stay on the right side and don't go into the attacking half of the field". Or, "You're a left winger, so stay on the left wing", or, "We're going to play 4–4–2 today". There might – and I say only *might* – be a case for something approaching those kind of instructions to a team of 19-year-olds playing for a regional championship. In terms of helping the development and understanding of a young soccer player, stick to "the basic unit is three". The player will far better appreciate and learn the principles of attacking play within the basic unit than in an undisciplined 11-a-side game.

Chapter 11
HELP! WE'RE UNDER ATTACK - DEFENSIVE SUPPORT

⚽ **SECTION I**

In terms of defending, soccer is the old cops and robbers game. The movies get it right every time. The scene is a locked apartment with a robber holing up inside. Outside, one cop says to the other, "I'm going in. You cover me!" And that, in a nutshell, is the art of defending in numbers. The cop charges in to make the first challenge but he is confident in the knowledge that his partner is behind him backing him up, covering, should it prove a bit more than he can handle.

In *illustration 251*, the "amateurs" have made the mistake of both going in at the same time to recover the "loot" (the ball) from the offender. Two doing one man's job may well lead to confusion, and both could be left thrashing at thin air as Mr. X makes his escape. In *illustration 252*, player 1 has moved in for the challenge but is covered a few yards behind by 2. Even if X is successful in avoiding the initial challenge of the first defender, he is set up for 2 to move in and finish the job off.

251   252

So much for cops and robbers and the "man advantage". Two players against one does happen frequently in the game, but because soccer is made up of equal numbers – whether it's five versus five or 11 versus 11 – we must look beyond the luxury of two defenders against one attacker.

Equal numbers
To mark or not to mark –
that is the question

Just look at the two versus two situation in *illustration 253*. The two white-shirted players are being tightly marked by defenders 1 and 2. The problem here is what happens if player 1 is beaten by the attacker dribbling past him? Defender 2 is in no position to cover his team mate

253

254

and so the attacker has a clear run at goal. You are probably thinking that if 2 moves to a covering position behind 1, the attacker off-the-ball is left unmarked. What should you do?

In a moment, I will suggest the answer. First, let me make it clear that I am not recommending any particular tactical method of defending. The covering and supporting positions in soccer remain basically the same whatever defensive system is being used – whether it be a zonal system or a man-marking system with a sweeper, English-style, Italian-style or Brazilian-style. It really makes no difference. So don't get caught up in the tactics game just yet. We are concerned here with an understanding of the defensive requirements of any defender in any part of the world – with any coach worth his salt!

So back to the two versus two situation and the answer.

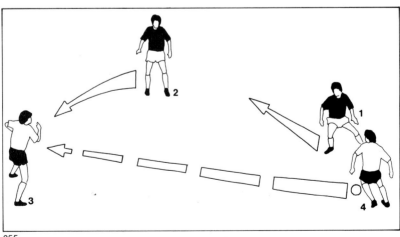

255

The half and half position

In *illustration 254*, defender 2 has come "on the cover" to a position at an angle to 1. That angle is normally close to a line from the ball to the defending goal. At the same time, defender 2 has not ignored player 3 and is in a "half-marking position" should the ball be passed by attacker 4 to his partner.

Remember – as *illustration 255* shows – that when the ball is played it will take some time for the pass to travel from one player to the other, plus normally another half-second or so for the ball to be controlled by the receiving player. During this time defender 2 has the chance to move across and close down player 3, and so take up a good marking position.

As 2 moves out to the challenge after the pass from player 4, it is just as important that defender 1 make the right recovery run. Defender 1 comes off 4 quickly to cover the challenging player – in this case, defender 2 – who, moments before, had been the covering player himself.

The recovery run

There is much more to the "recovery run" than has just been referred to in the "half and half" description. Whenever a player is *passed*, either by an attacking player or by the ball itself, he must immediately concern himself with his recovery run. There isn't a second to lose. All defenders must do everything possible to avoid two situations in particular. One is being caught on the "wrong side of the ball" – when the ball is between you and your defending goal. The other is being caught on the "wrong side of the man" – when an attacker has got in behind you and is nearer to the goal, but is still onside in the 11-a-side game.

256

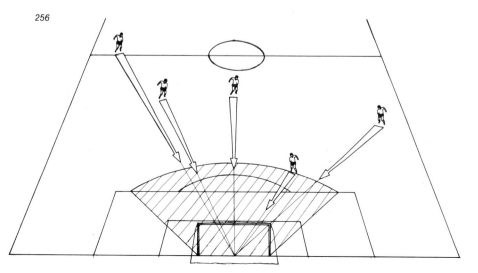

The golden rule is: when caught "wrong side", a player must immediately make a run on a line towards the middle of his defending goal – that is, towards the scoring zone (see Chapter 3, Shooting) – until he is back in a good defending position. (See *illustration 256*.) That doesn't mean the recovering defender must run all the way back into or around the penalty area – sometimes players recover too far, and waste energy without achieving good positioning. The main consideration is to be on the "right side" of both the opponent and the ball.

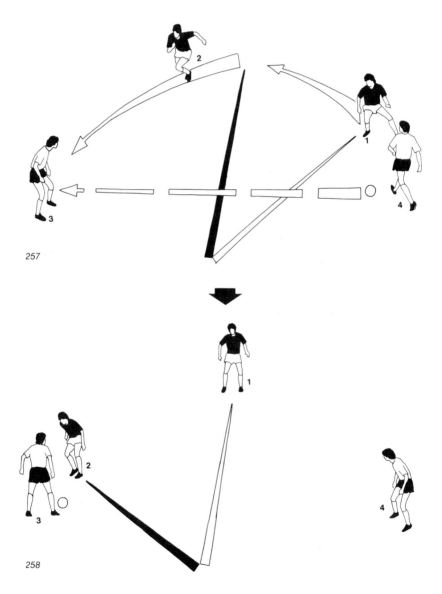

257

258

The pendulum

A pendulum swings backwards and forwards. *Illustrations 257 and 258*, our two versus two situation again, demonstrate the pendulum action of defenders: the closing down of the attacking player by one defender with the dropping-off movement of the other players at the same time, to put the cover on. Of course, the action won't ever be as smooth as a pendulum's – the coming forward and swing back action will very much depend on the actual situation presented to defenders by opposing players. But the pendulum comparison gives a good idea of the movement required.

An excellent and quick practice to get used to the pendulum is shown in *illustrations 257 and 258*, where attackers 3 and 4 are not allowed to move and defenders 1 and 2 are not allowed to tackle. So when the attackers decide to pass the ball, there is the defensive movement necessary to regain the right defending situation. The whole action is reversed again when the ball is played by 3 back to 4. Using a two-touch condition will allow enough practice and time to effect the marking and covering positions. Note the covering positions that the defenders take up when the ball is played away from the opponent who was being marked; these are achieved by means of a very quick recovery run into the half and half position. The practice is just a rehearsal to get the feel of what is required.

Defending against attackers as shown in *illustrations 257 and 258* and suggested in the practice should not be too difficult or at least not too complicated. But once the attackers start moving and particularly if they make diagonal and cross-over runs rather than moving straight up and down (see *illustration 259*), the problems greatly increase. Never-

259

theless the principle remains the same – one marking player for the opponent on the ball, one player giving cover.

Back chat

The scarcity of soccer players born with eyes in the backs of their heads makes it absolutely necessary for them to talk to one another. Players at the back of the defence, in covering positions, can act as the eyes for players in more advanced positions by offering such advice as "watch the number nine" or "move over to the right". The defender who is challenging the attacker with the ball needs precise information – "tackle him", "hold him up", "force him down the outside". The challenging defender has the task of watching both the man with the ball and the ball itself, which gives him little time to be looking around to see what else is happening. If he does, the player that the hustling defender is marking may well disappear in a flash. So "good talking" – clear and to the point, neither screaming nor whispering – is another important requirement of defensive support and should be practised.

Summary of defensive support

(See *illustration 260.*)

1. One player (1) should always be looking to go out and challenge for the ball. He should be encouraged to do so by the communications and instructions of his team mates.
2. The player going in to meet the attacker with the ball should be covered by a team mate (2) from behind (ideally five to seven yards

260

away) on a line between the ball and the defending goal.

3. The remaining defending players (3 & others) are then each concerned with three critical factors:

   a. Marking attackers in dangerous positions

   b. Giving extra cover to the hustler and the covering player

   c. Being ready and in position to move in and defend the area in front
of the goal (the scoring zone) – if they are not already in that particular zone.

   Note: As already pointed out, it may not be necessary or even wise to
recover back to the scoring zone. The 11-a-side game contains the
offside law, and offers tactical choices that sometimes make it more
effective not to retreat immediately into one's own penalty area.

   In Chapter 10, I said that the basic attacking unit is three. The
mimimum basic defending unit is two. Without a doubt, it is easier to
destroy than to create, and two capable defenders with a good understanding between them can make life very uncomfortable for three,
four, five – even six attackers. But like the attacking unit, the smallest
complete defensive unit is really three. One player can hustle and challenge, the second gives the immediate cover, and the third should provide the extra cover and double insurance that balances the defensive
trio. That third player assumes a valuable, stabilising role. He provides
the defensive anchor.

Practice 1

This practice requires three players and two balls. *Illustration 261*
shows traditional soccer-field markings but a playing area can be set
up anywhere. The attacker starts at a cone 15 yards from the penalty
area. The balls are placed 10 yards apart and 10 yards out from the

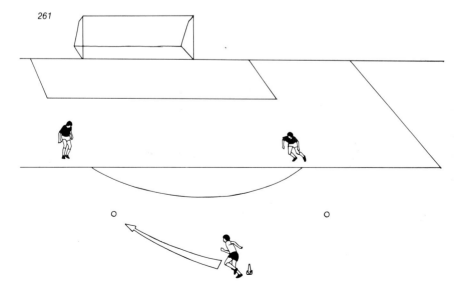

261

262

penalty area. The attacking player has one hand on the cone, or a foot in a small circle if a cone is not used. He can fake that he is going to move to one of the balls but the defender can leave the penalty area only when the attacker has actually moved off from the starting station. He decides which ball to go to, and then it becomes a one versus two situation with two defenders combining together to prevent a goal being scored.

If there is a fourth player, he can be used as the goalkeeper although one is not really necessary in this practice. The absence of a keeper is all the more reason why defenders should combine well to prevent the one attacker from even getting a shot at goal.

With three players, change around after 10 turns. The winning defensive duo is the pair that gives up the fewest goals. In individual competition the defender who concedes the fewest goals in his two defending sessions is the winner.

263

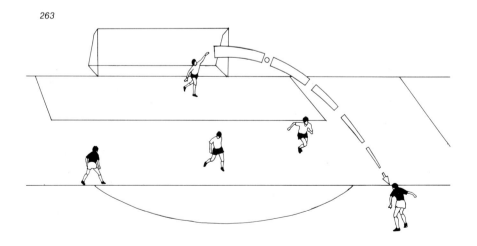

Practice 2

Once again, this is a simple two versus two game. It is a first-class situation for developing good defensive understanding, with an opportunity to get accustomed to the hustling and covering requirement (see *illustration 262*). In addition, the game emphasises the need for players to communicate with one another, particularly by talking. Better still, it's a real game of soccer and tremendously enjoyable!

Practice 3
Two versus two – shooting and defence

This shooting and defence exercise has been designed to provide practice in combined defending with the emphasis on accurate covering positions (see *illustration 263*).

The game actually works better with five or six players but can be adapted to other numbers. The goalkeeper throws the ball out beyond the penalty area and the two dark-shirted players attack the goal against the two defenders. Because the defending area in and around the penalty box is so critical, the covering defender must decide just how far he can afford to go in his covering. The attacker without the ball should never be granted so much space that a good pass would put him in the clear for a strike at goal. But the covering defender cannot leave his team mate uncovered in a one versus one. Rules such as how many attacks there will be per pair (say, 10) should be agreed upon beforehand. The winning duo is the pair conceding fewest goals.

SECTION II

It is important that the parent/coach does not get too involved in the technical detail if he is uncertain about the principles of defending. On the other hand, when asked a direct question, it may be very difficult to say, "I don't know". But it is honest. Don't be reluctant to say, "I'm not sure. I'll see if I can find out".

What has been explained up to now in this chapter is correct in terms of the *theory and the principles* involved in defending. But in a game situation, a difference of an inch or two in one direction or the other can be the factor that changes everything. It might be the spin of the ball, a fast or slow surface, even the wind. All these variables make "positional play" specific to the situation.

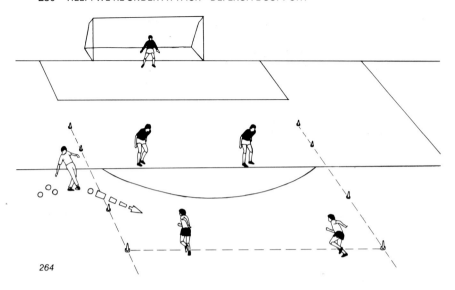

264

No book can deal with every contingency. Similarly, as a parent/coach, don't claim you have the answer unless you truly believe that you do.

The basic principles of defending will never change, and you can be confident in practising these with a young player. "Fault analysis" is different and very specific, so be careful!

Practice 4

As *illustration 264* shows, this practice involves a two versus two, along with a goalkeeper if numbers allow. (The coach can be the goalkeeper if there is a shortage of players, but be mindful that the control of the practice can be reduced in these circumstances.) A channel 15 yards

265

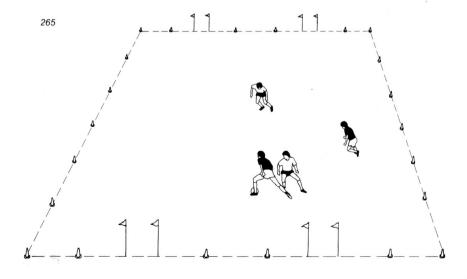

wide is marked in by lines of cones. The two attackers start in a position on the line between the first two markers, while the defenders must start from the edge of the penalty box. As soon as the coach plays the ball to either of the attackers, the practice becomes "live". If the coach is in goal, one of the attackers starts with the ball and it becomes "live" as soon as either one of the attackers moves off the starting line. The attackers do everything to get a strike at goal, but they have to stay inside the channel. The offside law applies – another good reason for the coach to be at the side of the channelled area.

This practice offers defenders (and attackers for that matter), first-class experience by making them aware of the value of the offside rule in relation to defending. The competitive aspect can be enhanced by each duo having six tries at defending; the pair that keeps goals and shots to a minimum wins. Suggest one point for a shot, two points for a goal.

Practice 5
The four goals game

This game is played in a 20-yard square (see *illustration 265*). The side with the ball can score in either of the attacking goals. The goals are two yards wide, four to five feet high. The practice situation compels players to take up good hustling positions. As well, they have to be completely accurate in covering positions, and cannot afford to leave any avenue open to either goal.

You can increase the value of the practice by drawing lines between the centre of the goals; these will give players "guide lines" to their hustling and covering positions. Mature players involved in 11-a-side games will take up positions and make recovery runs relative to the "clues" given on the field – the corner flags, centre circles, the D of the penalty area. In an authentic 11-a-side game, circumstances seldom allow a player the time to turn around and assess where the goal is in relation to his own position. Turning the head, even for a split second, may surrender the initiative, and the opponent will act at the moment of lost vision.

The two practices we have just covered will bring out most of the requirements of defensive support, but don't forget to consider the use of Practices 1, 2 and 3 with young players.

 **SECTION III**

Working in the basic units of defence – two's and three's – presents an organisation problem. To set up practices involving two versus two's

266

and three versus three's, requires more preparation and supervision than throwing the whole squad together in, say, a seven versus seven game. The coaching grid principle, as outlined in the Coaches' Segment, Chapter 2, and Chapter 10, Section III, can help enormously in this respect. So in spite of the organisational inconvenience, I would implore you to give young players ample opportunity to learn their defending in two's and three's. Don't confuse them (and possibly yourself) by attempting to deal with basic principles in the "greyness" of a number mass such as a six-a-side game.

The following practices will also help the organisational problem while giving players an opportunity to gain understanding through simple yet relevant situations.

Practice 6

Illustration 266 shows a simple three versus two situation. The coach, with a supply of balls on the half-way line, serves into each wave of three attackers who go for goal against the two defenders and the goalkeeper. The penalty area lines are extended by means of markers to "channel" that part of the field and so avoid unreasonably wide spaces for the two defenders to cover. Each set of three (the two defenders and a goalkeeper) must withstand a certain number of attacks – (8, 10, 12 –

however many the coach decides) – and then change with another group. The winning trio is the one conceding fewest goals.

Organisational Tip: Some numbers – such as 9's, 12's and 15's – work out nicely. The coach will only have the problem of deciding who goes in goal when it's the trio's turn to defend. But it *is* possible to work with such apparently awkward numbers as 10's, 11's, 13's and 14's. In the case of odd numbers, stay with groups of three but consider using one or two permanent goalkeepers – if there are two or more, they can work in rotation. Retain the two-defender situation but have the defenders take turns resting – so it becomes work two, rest one.

Practice 7

Illustration 267 shows a basic six-a-side but with a very important half-way line – *because players are not allowed to go over that line.* A suitably-sized area is marked out (about 50 x 40 yards) with goals (full-sized if available; improvised if not) and goalkeepers.

The players are positioned so that three attackers play against two defenders, with a goalkeeper in each half of the field. Players on the same team still combine together in spite of the half-way line rule – by passing to one another. The result is a real test of defensive technique and skill with three attackers versus two defenders in an active six-a-side game form.

Later on, the practice can be progressed, but only when the coach believes the players are ready for it. The progression is made by allowing one attacker to make a recovery run into the defending half of the field – but only after the ball has been played out of the recovering player's half. Once the attack has been repelled or – heaven forbid! – a

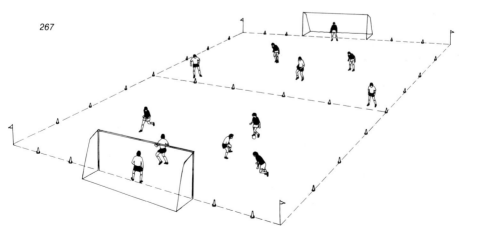

267

goal conceded, the player immediately returns into his own attacking half of the field once more.

Any attacker can make the recovery run, and making one run doesn't preclude that player from making the next one; however, if, as a result of a misunderstanding, two attackers move into the defending half at the same time, a penalty is conceded! Number juggling can take place according to the size of the squad. For example, an eight-a-side – four versus three – in two halves, plus goalkeepers, can be easily set up. Even a seven versus eight is possible: four versus two and four versus three plus goalkeepers, with the strongest defenders in the four versus two circumstances.

Practice 8
The 1, 2, 3 game

This game is the perfect one for combining all the requirements of defensive understanding (see *illustration 268*). A field is set up according to numbers and players' ages and ability (30 x 20 yards approximately). Goals are about two to five yards apart, depending on numbers in the goal zone. Even sides are selected, and a player on both sides is given a number from one to five (or however many players per team there are). The coach, with a supply of balls, positions himself on the side lines and rolls a ball into the field whenever and wherever he chooses, calling out any number from one to five. If it is "two", for example, the call brings out the two's from both teams who compete against one another in a one versus one situation. The rest of the team must remain in the goal zone and form a wall to defend against any shot – no handling. If you are unable to mark a zone in front of the goal, merely restrict the players in the wall to a maximum of 3 yards out of goal. If the ball goes out of play, the coach can roll in another ball for the same two opponents, or send them back to goal ready for the next number to be called out.

Now – and this is the fundamental part of the organisation – the coach, at any time while play is going on, can shout a second number resulting in a two versus two. And, if he wishes, a third number giving a three versus three. Any player failing to come out on the shout concedes a penalty to the opposition – a free shot at an open goal from the other goal, no goalkeepers. The calls may come at any time, and as rapidly as "2, 5, 3" if the coach so wishes.

This is a highly competitive game situation that requires total concentration and top-notch defending skills. It provides welcome practice in one versus one's, two versus two's and three versus three's. What's

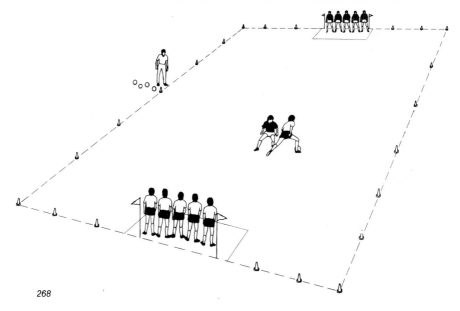

268

more, if a goal is conceded, the "culprit" can usually be identified and then must answer to his team mates. It goes without saying, this is a fast learning situation.

Summary

The three requirements of basic defensive understanding are:

1. Hustling the player with the ball
2. Covering the hustling player
3. Giving extra defensive cover, marking dangerous space and the players in that space, and by so doing, stabilising the defensive unit.

These requirements can best be learned in the relatively uncomplicated circumstances of one versus one's, two versus two's and three versus three's. Players exposed to the right learning situations will get the message very quickly.

Chapter 12
THE CREATION OF SPACE FOR ATTACKING PLAY

⚽ SECTION I

"Space" is the most exciting word in the English language today. Rocket ships, men on the moon, satellites...what next? "Space" is also the *most important* word in soccer, but you don't need a helmet, a special suit or an oxygen tank to get into it. There is plenty available on a soccer field – the trick is knowing how to use it and "create" it, particularly when the opposition is occupying the space you want.

Space and time go together in science fiction. In soccer, space *is* time. Let me give you a quick example to make that clear. A pass is played firmly towards a team mate. There is no opponent within 10 yards. If the control of the receiving player is sharp and accurate, and the ball is killed at his feet, the economical use of time to control the ball has given the space to now do something before the opposition can move in. However, if the control is poor and it takes three uncertain touches to finally bring the ball under control, then time has been lost and consequently space lost, too. Opponents will take the chance and the time to move in, mark, even tackle.

There are two main types of space that need to be considered: the space created by an individual for himself, and the space created by an individual for the benefit of the team.

1. The individual player creating space for himself

a. **Ball control:** good, sharp ball control, as we've already pointed out, buys time and space.

b. **Speed:** physical speed – the ability to run quickly with or without the ball will enable a player to gain space to receive a pass, or to move past players with the ball into space.

c. **Losing markers:** a player who is closely marked by an opponent is being denied space which makes it difficult for him to receive the ball. The trick is to lose that opponent and so gain the space in which to receive the ball. The marked player's big advantage is that it is *he* who decides when to move. The marker can only "read" what to do. Therefore, no matter how alert the marking defender is, he will always be reacting to the decision of the marked player and can be caught off-guard.

Players can work on the following four "tricks" with friends or else incorporate them into their practice sessions.

Coming off the defender

In *illustration 269*, the attacker without the ball – although tightly marked by the defender – comes off the defender at the last split second and

269

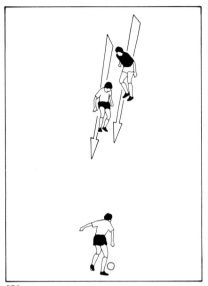

270

moves out three to five yards to receive the ball from his team mate. Not only has the receiving player come off the defender but he has chosen to *move out at an angle*: this gives him a side position enabling him to see both the ball coming in and the defender's reaction to his move. It is risky for the defender, because of the angle of the player receiving the ball, even to think about challenging as it will be difficult to make contact with the ball. If he does attempt to tackle, he could easily "sell" himself in his anxiety to win the ball. This will mean not only an unsuccessful tackle but his losing out on the action as he is bypassed by player and ball.

Spin and go

Illustration 270 shows the opposite trick at work. The attacking player entices the defender towards the ball by moving casually towards his own player. He then quickly spins and utilises the space now created behind the defender to allow his partner to chip or play the ball into his run.

Run, check, come back

Running with the apparent intention of receiving a through-ball forces the defender to go with the attacking player (see *illustrations 271 to*

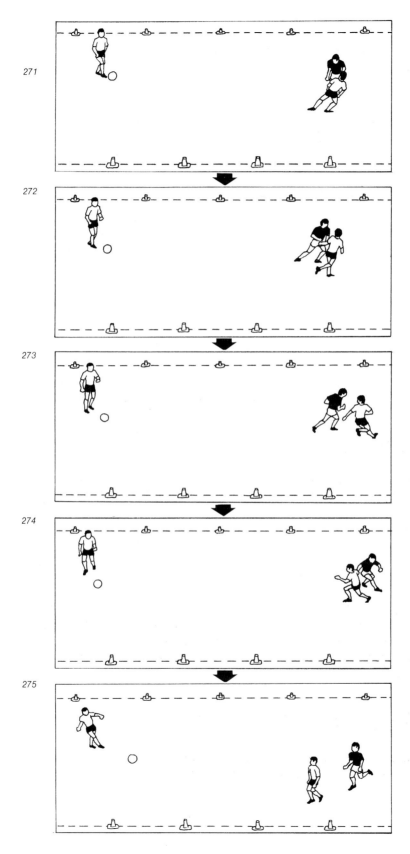

271

272

273

274

275

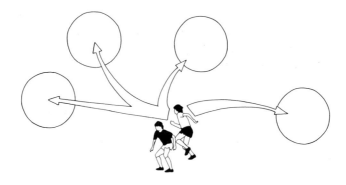

276

275). (In the 11-a-side game, the defender may try to take advantage of the offside rule, so be careful.) The attacking player is then able to "check" and come back to receive the ball, leaving the defender still applying the brakes well after the attacking player has made his decision.

Blind side of opponents

Any run or movement outside of the defender's vision gives the attacker an advantage. Remember that the defender must also concentrate on where the ball is at all times, so he cannot watch everything *at the same time*. The moment a player is out of the defender's vision is the time that player should move into space to receive the ball. In *illustration 276* the attacking player, having got on the back side or "blind side" of the defender, has the opportunity to move into several different spaces.

2. Creating space for the team and for team mates

One particular teacher I worked with back in Lancashire, Brian Morgan, had a one-word cry every time a player won the ball from the opposition: Spread. He was a Welshman with a resounding baritone voice that made the word sound something like "S p r-r-r-e-e-e-a-d!"

That teacher was definitely on the ball. When the opposition has possession, players inevitably and with good reason group tightly together to win the ball back from the opposition. But it results in too many players remaining around the ball when possession is won back. Having won back the ball, the requirement is space, and spreading provides the room to attack. As well – almost as if by magic – when the attacking side spreads, so does the opposition. Thus space is created.

Look at *illustration 277* where, in a simple two versus two, the two attackers are almost handshaking distance apart. The two defenders have been helped in their task, as they also are able to stay close together, defending the ball and the route to goal.

277

278

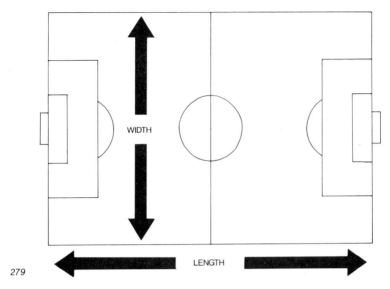

279

However, in *illustration 278*, the attacking player off-the-ball has made a run using the full width of the area and has moved slightly forward of his team mate with the ball. Now the covering defender has a real problem. Does he move and give close attention to the wide attacker but then leave his team mate almost in a one versus one situation? Or does he stay in a good covering position and give the space of an easy pass to the wide player? The dilemma has been caused by spreading on the part of the player off-the-ball.

So, using my Welsh friend's terminology, the following possibilities for spreading are available to all attacking players.

Use of width

The width of the field or practice area is the total space from one side line to the other. The length is the space end to end from goal line to goal line (see *illustration 279*).

Using the width of the field is probably *the* major consideration in attacking tactics. I am not talking about playing orthodox wingers in the team, although the wing position (left or right) is one which does recognise the importance of width. The plain fact is that *all* players must be aware of the consideration of width and be prepared to use it.

In *illustration 278*, you can see what happens in a simple two versus two situation when one attacker takes advantage of available width. The defenders are immediately put under pressure and "stretched".

In *illustration 280*, we have used a four versus four game, where the attacking side is positioned to support their player with the ball in terms

280

281

of providing good passing angles. But because they have not used the full width available to them, the opposition find it easy to form a compact defending unit.

In *illustation 281*, 3 has pulled fully wide on the right and attacker 4 has moved out onto the left. While the passing angles from player 1 to his three team mates have hardly altered:

a. The chances of any pass being intercepted have been decreased
b. The likelihood of the attackers being tackled on receiving a good pass has greatly decreased
c. And the defensive unit is being pulled apart with "holes" opening up.

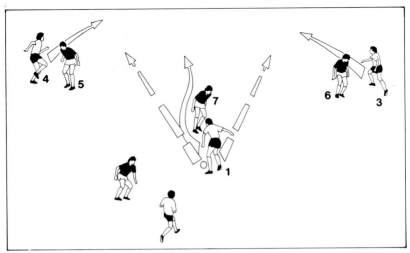

282

Why? 5 and 6 have been forced, by the positions of 3 and 4, to move out into half and half defending positions as described in Chapter 11. They really cannot go all the way out into a tight marking position without surrendering the cover. So there is space to make the pass. In the unlikely event that defenders 5 and 6 choose to tight-mark the wide players – which is not advisable – space is created behind the hustling defender (7). This gives 1 the choice of either taking on defender 7 and dribbling past with no covering players, or playing the ball behind and inside the wide positioned defenders (see *illustration 282*), thus allowing attacking players 3 and 4 in the wide positions to move on diagonal runs into the space created.

Illustration 282 shows the attacking space created by the good wide positions of players 3 and 4 and the poor marking positions of players 5 and 6. But whether the defenders are in questionable tight-marking positions or good covering positions, they have been stretched by the attacking team's sound use of width. In other words, whatever the defenders do, they are at a disadvantage as a result of attackers utilising width.

Use of length

1. **Pushing back the defence:** When being marked by a defender, it is a good idea for an attacker just to walk away. It's quite amazing how many defenders will insist on accompanying the player. It can be like

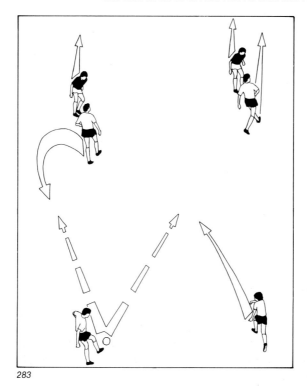

283

taking a trained dog for a walk – he will stay at "heel". Defenders can be walked – or run – into poor defending positions. In a regulated 11-a-side game, many defenders will actually forget the protection they have from the offside rule and still get walked back towards their own goal.

Using the weakness of this defensive characteristic, space can be opened up as shown in *illustration 283*. Players, having walked their markers away, are able to come off to receive the ball in the space created, and combine together to make an attack on goal. Alternatively, players in the team may use the space that has been created by the front players walking away the defenders. (Shown here by the player in the bottom right-hand corner moving into the space created.) So taking defenders away creates space in front of defences to be utilised:

    a. to receive passes from team mates in deeper positions, or

    b. for other team mates coming forward from a midfield position to move in to receive the ball.

2. **Drawing defenders in:** Because defenders can be walked almost anywhere you please, space can be created behind the defence by drawing defenders too close towards the opponent with the ball. In

284

285

illustration 284, the defenders are in good positions but in *285*, because 2 and 3 have come towards 1 who has the ball – faking their desire for a pass – the two covering defenders have been drawn in with them. This creates space behind the three defenders which enables either 2 or 3 or both to spin and go towards the goals, with player 1 able to slide through a pass into the paths of either attacker.

Alternatively, if this were a game, another player could make a run from the back and steal through the defence into the space behind the defending players.

Mobility – or plain, old-fashioned running

An attacker who is always running, seeking good attacking positions for himself, or dragging defenders out of covering positions to make space for his team mates, very quickly loses his popularity – with the opposition. They hate it. As soon as an opponent starts moving – with the opponent's team in possession of the ball, of course – the opposition's defence is left with a problem. Do they go with the running player and leave a hole in the defence or do they leave him unmarked with a chance perhaps of a free route to goal? The more running an attacker does, the more anxious the opposition becomes, because of the greater number of problems posed.

In *illustration 286*, 2 has made an overlap run behind 1 and into a wide position down the right side. Player 4 has made a flat run, i.e., sideways – threatening the blind sides of 5, 6 and 8; 4 ends up in a wide position on the left touch line.

286

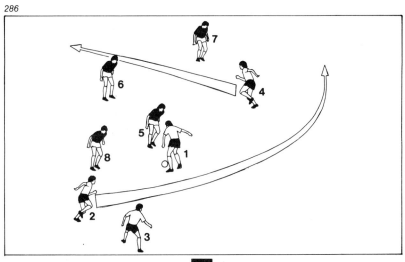

287

Illustration 287 shows that all the defenders have been forced to make decisions, whether they like it or not. Defender 5, for instance, has decided to stay marking the man with the ball (1) and in this situation, he is right. Defender 8 has decided he needs to do something about 2's overlap run and is moving across to cover him. However, 7 has been dragged over by the initial run of 4. The illustration shows that neither 7 nor 6 has decided who will mark 4 as defender 6 continues to hold his covering position of the hustling defender (5). Consequently, at the moment captured in the illustration, neither 6 nor 7 is effectively marking attacker 4. The four defenders have been pulled together by the runs of players 2 and 4, thus opening up a big chunk of attacking space for 2 in particular to exploit. Player 1 with the ball only has to play a simple pass into the path of 2's run.

Now, of course, the defenders *don't* have to make the decisions that have been indicated in this example. And obviously, it would have been far better for them if one or two hadn't. But they *are* forced to make decisions in this situation whether they want to or not. **And if the individual decisions of all four defenders are not in harmony, the defensive unit is in big, big trouble.**

Summary

Remember that each player in the team is an attacker when his team has possession of the ball but by the same rule, all players are required to

288

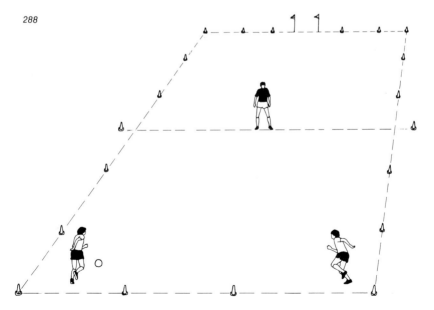

act as defenders in one form or another when their team has lost possession.

So all attacking players are "space men". Creating space to exploit the opposition is the number one tactical consideration of attacking play. Keep these factors in mind and apply them in the following recommended practices.

As with the practices in Chapters 10 and 11, "creation of space" practices need at least two co-operating players and one defender.

Practice 1

This is a two versus one and makes use of a 20 x 10 yard area containing a three-yard goal (see *illustration 288*). The attackers start in the opposite corners at the far end of the goal – one with the ball. The defender must position himself in the middle of the area on an imaginary centre line; that line is marked by the two cones, each one yard outside the practice area. Either of the attacking players can make the first move out of the corners, with or without the ball. This starts the practice, at which stage the defender can move anywhere and do anything within the rules to prevent a goal from being scored. The practice ends when a goal is conceded or the ball goes out of play.

Each person has his 10 tries at defending. The players total up the goals scored in their two attacking "sets" so it's twice 10 tries at attacking, and one times 10 at defending.

A further scoring rule can be added if you so wish. Should the defender win the ball and maintain possession, then instead of playing the ball indiscriminately out of the area and so finishing that particular attack, he can try to score a bonus point by hitting either of the two centre point marker cones placed one yard outside the area. The bonus points are added to the goals total. The defender must be careful, however, that he does not risk losing the ball himself in his quest for a bonus point.

Practice 2

Illustration 289 shows a simple two versus two with goals set four to six feet wide. Practice 2 differs from other two versus two games only in the size of the field required. It is suggested that a fairly large "area" (25 yards long x 20 yards wide) be set up. This should encourage players to work skilfully to take advantage of the space available. Still, that extra room can be utilised only by players who are willing to employ the methods discussed in this chapter. As they become more proficient, the size of the playing area can be tightened up.

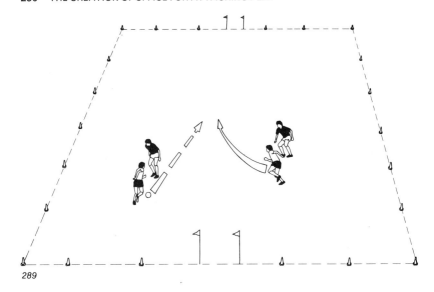

289

🏐🏐 SECTION II

Practice 3

Begin by setting up a 30 x 10 yard rectangle, with a goal four yards wide, five feet high and 10 yards beyond the end line (see *illustration 290*). The coach takes position on any side of the practice area, but should change over every so often. When he gives the word "go", the attacker attempts to "lose his marker" by faking the defender, or by getting on the "blind side", or by "drawing in" the defender and attempting to use the space behind, or by any of the other methods we have discussed. However, the coach can play the ball in only **when the attacker asks for it**. The attacking player, on receiving the ball, can shoot for goal at any stage – even with his first touch if he so chooses – as long as he is within the rectangular area. The defender, therefore, cannot afford to stand off or he will make it too simple for the attacking player.

Each player has five tries, the winner being the highest scorer. This is a very demanding activity, so give the players a breather between turns. Don't forget to alternate the side for serving the ball, as players do develop a tendency to favour their natural foot. Encourage them both verbally and by the service, in this case, to use both feet.

Practice 4

Illustration 291 clearly demonstrates that the two attackers will have to play very well together to get past the defenders while remaining within

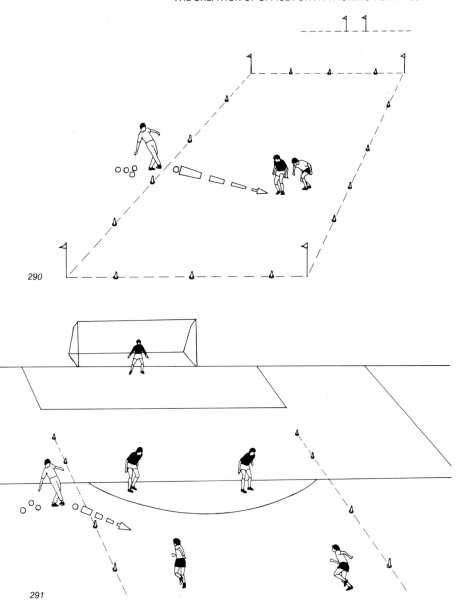

290

291

the 12-yard-wide corridor – particularly as the coach should be applying the offside rule. Use a two versus one situation if you are working with only three; with larger numbers, split up into pairs. The competitive aspect can be introduced in the same way as has been suggested in other similar practices: points for goals, a running total kept by each individual.

SECTION III

Space is what attacking play is all about, but a lack of practice space can be a major headache for the coach. Here again, I recommend that you adopt the coaching grid principle and take advantage of whatever space and equipment is available.

Coaching players on how to open up attacking space, both for themselves and for the team, requires a high level of soccer knowledge. So you need to be careful. The simple principles outlined in this chapter can, and should, be demonstrated to the players – but having to advise youngsters on specific problems that crop up in practice or in games is more difficult. **You must be sure of your facts and your analysis before attempting to suggest corrective action.** Proceed cautiously, or stated another way, "if in doubt, say nowt". Fault analysis will test the world's greatest coaches, never mind the amateur.

Without a doubt, defenders are affected and confused by the runs of attacking players, whether the attackers go forward, backward, sideways, on diagonal runs, curving runs, out to the touch lines, or to the backs of the defences. As soccer is a team game, the "herd" instinct is very much in evidence and often gets players into trouble. Defenders are used to being a cohesive unit and tend to react "together". They will even react "collectively" to the movement of one opponent!

Geoff Hurst, the three-goal hero of England's 1966 World Cup success, tells a story about when he was travelling with the England squad a few years back. On one occasion, the team had a two-hour layover at a European airport, and passed the time by sitting in the airport lounge reading, drinking coffee and playing cards. Hurst needed to go to the lavatory, so off he went and six of the England team followed him! Just how factual that story is I don't know, but soccer players *are* drawn by movement and *do* tend to stick together!

Team practices should be set up to give players experience in the creation and exploitation of space. Include in the team session those practices outlined in Sections I and II of this chapter, developed in organisational terms to accommodate the greater numbers.

Practice 5

This practice involves four-a-side play, as shown in *illustration 292* and makes use of more players in a specific situation than most of the other practices we've dealt with so far. Working for space within a 40 x 35 yard area – with goals two yards wide and four feet high, and the no-handling rule should, in effect, give players ample opportunity to apply all they have learned in this chapter. The four versus four situation can

292

293

also be used in the tournament format outlined in Chapter 10 (with four players participating instead of three).

Practice 6
Attack versus defence

Illustration 293 shows an attacking unit of four players opposite four defenders in one half of the field. The coach serves the ball in from the centre circle and the attackers attempt to get a strike at goal. The defenders' first priority is to destroy the attacking efforts but if they win the ball and maintain possession, they can score in either of the two small goals positioned on the half-way line (the goals are four yards apart). All aspects of creating space should be employed in this practice if the attackers are to win the duel. Scoring should be one point for each goal the defending unit scores in the small goals on the half-way line, four points for an authentic goal from the attacking group. The winning group is the unit scoring the most points.

Practice 7

As you can see in *illustration 294* the half-way line here becomes the boundary for all players. The ball can move the whole length of the field, but the players cannot. So a four versus four situation is established in each half of the field: the four attackers try to link with the four defenders in the other half by means of passing the ball. The same applies to the other team. In all other respects, the rules are the same as those of the conventional 11-a-side game.

The area of the field may well have to be adjusted depending on the age and size of the players. In the example shown, the field is 40 yards wide x 60 long. One thing is certain; the half-way line rule forces attacking players in each half to work hard and skilfully to create space into which the ball can be played and received from the back half.

Summary

In Chapters 10, 11 and 12, we have shifted our emphasis from individual skill considerations to a greater understanding of the game – how

294

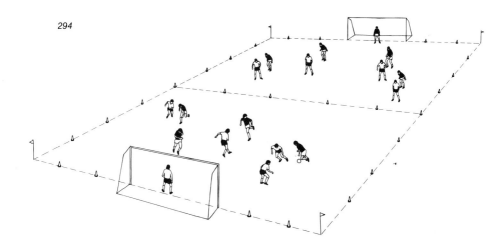

players can co-operate with each other to become an effective unit. A very meaningful saying in soccer is that "a successful team performance is always greater than the sum of the individual parts". That, of course, should be the objective but unless those individual parts are skilled, all the cohesion, understanding and team spirit players can muster will count for little – in fact, will not exist. It is not a chicken and egg situation. What comes *first* is the development of a soccer player's ability to kick, head, control and win the ball.

Learning the fundamentals of the game should never be drudgery. It should be total enjoyment, and this can be achieved by *playing* the game of soccer – in practice.

FOR THE COACHES

Introduction

Coaching soccer is a most humbling experience, no matter what the level. I've had the privilege of coaching the whole spectrum of players – from six-year-olds to hard-bitten professionals, from women's teams to men representing their country in professional world championships. Just remember that no one possesses all the answers. There has never been the perfect coaching session yet!

In my experience, the most challenging group of players to work with is the youth team. The younger the players, the more the problems. Now before you stop reading, throw the book away and resign your position, let me hasten to add that coaching youngsters also has to be the most rewarding experience a coach could hope for.

There are any number of physical difficulties that you, as a coach, will encounter and be obliged to cope with – poor facilities, limited equipment, lack of proper field markings, maybe even having to share your practice area with another group. Consider the organisation and setting-up of practices, and the many idiosyncracies and inconsistencies in personality that are often more evident in younger players. Despite the many variables, there do exist some reliable guidelines that can guarantee success to the team practice – if they are observed.

This segment of the book should be read from start to finish by the team coach, and I would strongly recommend that an enthusiastic parent do the same. Even though the emphasis is on conducting team practice, the techniques for teaching remain fundamentally the same – even when coaching your son and two of his friends. After reading this segment, the coach can refer back to whatever chapter is appropriate for his next team session.

Before conducting any practice at whatever level of ability or accomplishment, the coach must do his homework or the result may be a pretty superficial learning session.

Besides the initial **planning and preparation** of the session, the coach must always be aware of the **needs of the team** – although normally they are predictable and fairly constant, like the necessity to practise passing and ball control. **Facilities and equipment** vary from excellent to mediocre to downright desperate! They need to be taken into consideration and, if necessary, improved – which can often be done surprisingly easily and cheaply.

Conducting the team practice itself can be a daunting prospect. Generally, one hour should be long enough for a practice but occasionally, players will feel cheated if they don't have at least a 90-minute, or even a two-hour, session. "How am I going to occupy the team for that length of time?" is your desperate thought. Again, intelligent planning and organisation are your most effective tools.

With the right spirit and atmosphere, you are in business. One word of warning, however, about "over-preparation". Having too many practices to cover during the session is almost – but not quite – as bad as having too few. Over-preparation can result in the coach moving from one practice to another without achieving any improvement, and worse, without giving the players a real opportunity to practise. This will frustrate them and they will quickly lose their concentration.

As well, I would appeal to all coaches – whatever their experience – **not to attempt to be "clever" but to be honest**. There is no harm in admitting that you don't know all the answers. Don't risk losing the respect of your players by trying to bluff it.

"Improvisation" must become a key word for young enthusiasts. Most of the great soccer players of the past have come from the lower economic groups. Few could afford proper equipment, and if you were the kid on the block with a soccer ball, you automatically won the popularity poll.

It was a standing joke in Britain in the 1930s that when a professional club was short of a goal-scorer, a coach would go and whistle down the nearest mineshaft and up would pop three ready-made centre forwards. And, of course, what was true of Britain was true of the whole of Europe. Any waste ground became a soccer field and was prepared by the youngsters themselves. Jackets became goals and roads became touch lines. Many a two versus two or three versus three game was improvised in the back alleys of the industrial cities.

Things have changed since those days but it's still interesting to consider the circumstances that produce outstanding soccer players. Think of Brazil, which presents to the world players of unbelievable skill. What happens in these environments is that youngsters play soccer in small quarters where tight skill is very much encouraged by the limitations of the "field". No one is suggesting that coaches should revert to these circumstances if better facilities exist. What is being emphasised is that fancy equipment or ideal playing conditions are not as important as providing the learning situation for young players.

The practices that have been assembled in this book will aid players in developing their skills and improving their role as effective team members. All the practices have been proven; most are used regularly at the very highest levels of the game, but have been selected here because they are just as appropriate for any age and degree of accomplishment, and are particularly timely for young players.

This segment will help the coach deal with some of the less predictable situations that may arise during the team practices ... how to cope with uneven numbers when splitting the team into group activities; what disciplinary sanctions to employ without affecting team spirit and morale; what to do when a practice is simply not working.

From the question of long-term coaching programmes to the problems surrounding transportation and fund-raising for equipment, the soccer coach must address a host of sport-related subjects, and this segment should cover a good many bases.

So if you have never played the game and have never coached, don't be put off. There are plenty of suggestions on how to conduct the team practice in this segment, and enough practices in Chapters 1 to 12 to ensure your success. If you know next to nothing about the game, you may even be at an advantage, certainly in comparison to those know-it-alls. At the very least, you will bring to soccer an enquiring and open mind – a most valuable quality in coaching.

Chapter 1
COACHING AND TEACHING METHODS

There are certain fundamental considerations which should not be ignored by the coach. These are simple and once understood require, in the main, only the application of common sense.

1. Dress

Turning out in a mud-splattered sweatshirt 30 years out of date, and with a hole in the knee, might guarantee a few laughs but not too much else. You are the coach and should look the part. You don't have to be flamboyant, but a smart and clean, athletic appearance – even if you are a few pounds overweight – will give a favourable impression, and get the session off on the right foot.

2. Manner

This is "you". Don't even think of trying to be anyone else. All too often a coach models himself on his hero – with disastrous effects. Of course you can, and should, modify your manner and personality to suit the situation and particularly the age of the group. **A sense of humour** in

259

any situation can work wonders – and believe me, you need one to be a soccer coach! **Patience** is another important advantage because progress at any level is only made slowly. But don't mistake patience and tolerance for softness and sloppiness. A coach who's a pushover is not doing his players a favour. You'll probably find the real "you" is fine and only needs some fine tuning.

3. Voice

You need to know your own voice – what it's capable of, what it can't do. Sounding like a drill sergeant on the soccer field may appear to be an advantage but quite frankly, it's hardly essential. "Noisy teacher, noisy class" is a saying I recall from my teacher training days. At the same time, talking so quietly that you appear almost to be apologising for your presence is not good either. Assess your own voice, and adjust your approach accordingly. If it's quiet, bring the group in, should you need to address them all and then speak to them softly, clearly, and confidently. If you have a loud voice, learn to moderate it in personal, one-to-one situations, but be sure to take advantage of it when your players are spread all over the field. With a big voice, you won't have to bring the group in to make yourself understood.

4. Position of the coach and position of the group

A bit of "native cunning" is required (that's another expression for common sense!) when dealing with the following factors:

Wind

Shouting against the wind can be a futile effort. If there is a strong breeze, use it – don't fight it. Take up your position wherever possible so that the wind will carry your voice. Or bring the group in so that they can all hear you and clearly understand.

Sun

On clear days – particularly in the early morning, late afternoon and early evening – the sun can become a real hazard to visibility. With the sun behind you, **your** view of the players may be fine, but theirs is impaired. Bear this factor in mind when conducting the practice session and in particular, when bringing the group in for a demonstration or a brief huddle.

The huddle

Ideally players should be kept active without lengthy group pow-wows. After all, young players want to play, not talk. They don't care to spend much time listening and certainly have no desire for lectures. However, when you need to get a point across, demonstrate a particular aspect of the practice, or change an exercise, it will become necessary to bring the group in. At these times, several points should be kept in mind.

a. Keep the group in a compact unit – **in front of you**. If they are allowed to drift to the side or behind you, you will be unable to see them properly and therefore unable to assess their reaction, their concentration and their interest.
b. Encourage the players to come into the huddle quickly – "last one in does 10 push-ups". This will prevent players from drifting in casually. Otherwise, the momentum of the session slows down, and valuable practice and playing time is lost.
c. Insist that the balls be pushed to one side, away from the players. No one can resist the attraction of a ball, particularly if there is one at his feet. The huddle should be brief and to the point – and anything that distracts the players will lessen its impact.

5. Importance of demonstration

"A picture is worth a thousand words". A cliché, true, but so appropriate when discussing skills learning. It should be the catch-phrase of all soccer coaches. Demonstration is easily **the most important single tool in soccer learning**.

The use of demonstration should **not** be limited merely to "showing" how particular skills are performed, or displaying ways of exploiting certain soccer situations. Demonstration should also be freely used to give a "picture" of how a practice should be organised and how it will function. Try to explain to a youngster in words how to ride a bike. Then *show* him without a single word, and he will get the idea right away. He may still not be able to ride the bike, but that's where the practical coaching comes in. There are a number of different ways to use demonstration.

1. **The coach demonstrates:** If you are an ex-player and a fairly good performer, there is no better demonstrator than yourself. You can show what is required and gain respect at the same time. On the other hand, you may not have been a very good player. Don't worry about it. I understand the problem, as I was a goalkeeper, but limited in many outfield skills. There are several alternatives.

    a. You can be bold, have a try, and at least give the players something of an idea. Then maybe demonstrate further in slow-motion, emphasising the key factors.

    b. If you are very unsure about this, then demonstrate in slow-motion, outlining the requirements. While it's practically impossible to simulate the mechanisms of certain techniques or skills in slow-motion, the idea will at least have been shown.

    c. In a group situation, such as a two versus two, use the "walk-through" method. This is the same as the "slomo" technique, where the coach walks through the sequence and asks other players to walk through as well, to demonstrate what is required. By a combination of demonstration and explanation, the idea is communicated to the players.

When using the walk-through technique, make sure all key points are explained and if possible, demonstrated. For example, how is the opposition likely to react to the moves, and what are the alternatives if the opponents don't react as anticipated?

Be certain everyone understands that all positions are related to where the ball is at any given time. So as you walk through, adjust the position of the ball, or at least verbally make your players realise that the ball's position is usually changing.

2. **Use of individual players or groups:**

    a. *A youngster* whom you know to have the ability to perform the skill in question can be the best demonstrator of all, giving the rest of the group something to aspire to as well as motivating them to attain the same standards and recognition. If one of their team mates can do it, so can they. But be careful that the same player is not always used in the demonstration, or the motivational effect can quickly be lost. The "superstar" gets big-headed and his team mates become resentful.

    b. *Using one group* to demonstrate to others can have many advantages – particularly if that group is performing a drill or practice very well, or for that matter, poorly. The group is used as a model for the others. As well, if you want to progress the practice by introducing another consideration or modification, a central demonstration by one reasonably accomplished and receptive group will generally implant the idea and allow the team practice to continue.

3. **Other instructional/visual aids:** Films, video and audio cassettes,

books, slides, blackboards and charts all have a part to play in demonstrating techniques. But don't let them become a steady diet. Remember – youngsters learn by doing, and with limited time available, the best place for learning is on the practice field. Demonstration is the essence of soccer coaching. Show them quickly and clearly what is wanted, and then let them get on with it.

As a professional coach and a player, the most demoralising chant I have ever heard from the fans is "Boring, boring, boring!" Be very careful you don't earn that chant – or its equivalent – from your young charges. I can guarantee that too much talk, too much standing about, and too little action will bring about just that response. **Show them as quickly as you can and then let them play**.

6. Climate and field conditions

Always be mindful of the physical conditions of the playing field: is it ankle-deep in mud, rock-hard from frost or sun, rutted by poor maintenance? Climate and temperature must be taken into account. A practice session on a freezing field or in tropical temperatures, or in driving rain, should be handled quite differently on all three counts.

Some weather conditions can be anticipated, others cannot. Nevertheless, **all can be planned for**, which means flexibility on the part of the coach. **Contingency planning** is essential. The very word "contingency" means that plans can't be hard and fast. But there are certain guiding principles worth bearing in mind. For instance, we all know if it is wet and cold, the key is **activity** – short, sharp and snappy. Keep the session moving, intensify the activity, and reduce the length of the workout.

Conversely, if it is a really hot day, the intensity of the session may have to be reduced using, for example, skills practices which require a high level of technique and touch but are not overly demanding physically. Practising controlling the ball in pairs, using chest or thigh, is one possibility. And games such as change-soccer give a welcome break to the players.

Inflexible people with inflexible plans are a hazard in almost any circumstance, but so are the off-the-cuff, laid-back characters. The answer, very clearly, lies in striking a happy medium – thorough preparation but with an awareness and a preparedness to change when conditions change.

7. Modifying the practices

This is perhaps the most difficult area for the coach. Plans on paper may turn out to be very different in reality, e.g. the 20 × 20 yard area for the three versus one practice proves to be far too big for nine-year-olds. The thinking seemed right but the reality was wrong. What do you do? Obviously, you change it. No matter what the inconvenience – or the embarrassment – if it's not working, you must adjust the practice.

The following is a mental checklist for the coach to run through whenever a practice is not proceeding smoothly:

1. Is the space wrong? Is it too long, too wide, too short, too narrow? Are the goals too wide, too narrow?
2. Are the rules too restrictive? Is one-touch too difficult? Is two-touch?
3. Are the numbers of players right for the practice? Two versus one may be too ambitious at this time – should it be modified to three versus one? Note that the problem might be alleviated by adjusting your space (see [1]), but if the space is too small or too big, it may be easier and quicker to change the numbers rather than reorganise the playing area.

Human beings move more readily than cones, posts or lines. So if three versus one in a 20-yard square isn't working out, consider four versus two rather than reducing the size of the practice area.
4. Is the practice too difficult? Too easy?
5. Are there some organisational points that were overlooked in the initial setting up of the practice? Are the players wearing identifying bibs? Are they clear as to how points or goals are scored? Do they understand the objectives? If there is any suggestion of confusion, stop the session and explain, or better still, demonstrate.
6. Has the demonstration or explanation of the practice been fully understood? If in doubt, repeat the demonstration and obtain feedback to indicate an understanding.

"Changing horses in midstream" is one of the least attractive situations a coach can face. It may be embarrassing. But you cannot afford to worry about that – no one's perfect. You also can never be sure that it's going to work the second time around! **But if it's not working, you have to change it or abandon it**.

After modifying the practice, if it is still not working, you have a judgement call to make. Do you adjust again? Or do you go into a fall-back position? And don't be afraid of the latter. Buy time! There will be many practices which you have introduced previously that have become an established, accepted, and enjoyable part of most sessions. Now is the time to use them. Your next decision must be whether to return to the particular practice that has failed to work with further fine tuning at some future date. Only *you* know that answer. The observation I would make is that young and old admire persistence – so don't be put off too easily.

These kinds of decisions are never easy to make. Experience often gives you the composure, the insight and the answers with regard to modifying practices. Be honest, and level with your players. If you cannot make it work, admit it – and don't try to bluff your way out. Instead, look for solutions and alternatives.

8. The numbers game

I referred in the previous section to modifying practices if they are not working properly, and suggested increasing the numbers if the area was too big. By the same rule, one would consider reducing the numbers if the marked areas were too restricting. But the space may be exactly right, and still the practice is not functioning. At this point you may need to consider some changes in the numbers.

In most cases, the number problem occurs when there is opposition present. If you are working on an aspect of attacking play and the defence has little or no problem stopping the attack, then it is certainly worth considering reducing the number of defenders or increasing the number of attackers. For example, in a three versus three situation, if the three attackers are not posing any problems to the three defenders, consider bringing in an additional attacker to make it four versus three.

Or alternatively try taking away a defender to make it three versus two. When success is achieved, return to the original three versus three.

When the numbers involved are not working out, don't be afraid of having some players standing on the side lines. The secret obviously is to do everything possible to maintain their interest and keep them involved. There are several ways of doing that:

1. Change the players at regular intervals so that no one is left out too long – but don't change too frequently or it will become a merry-go-round with virtually no practice time.
2. Organise another unsupervised activity that the players out of the main practice can involve themselves in, such as a three versus three game.

If you do have a secondary activity taking place, try to set it up in an area where it won't distract the main group. And don't leave the unsupervised players to their own devices for too long!

Discipline and sanctions

We would all like to think that every youngster is so enthusiastic about soccer practice that there will be no control problems, but we know that's unrealistic. When I first became a father, I asked a friend – a more experienced dad – what was the secret of bringing up children. He replied, "A mixture of compassion and discipline – but don't ask me what the mix is!".

Without question, the qualities we've already mentioned – enthusiasm, patience, a sense of humour – are essential in establishing the right atmosphere. Blending thorough preparation with the enjoyment factor will greatly reduce the potential problem. But discipline will still be needed to keep the group moving in the right direction.

The following is a list of points that will help in the "mix".

1. **Praise:** Nothing works better than a little encouragement and recognition, particularly when constructive criticism is so fundamental to improving performance and ironing out faults. Praise will inspire, or at worst – sweeten the pill, and neutralise the criticism.

2. **Incentives:** One successful youth coach in England attributed all his success to jellybeans which he carried in his tracksuit trouser pocket. There was much more to his technique than that, but rewarding the best teams, the best individual performance and the best "triers" with fruit, sweets or soft drinks can keep most young players "on-side".

3. **"Kiddology":** Tongue-in-cheek "threats", challenges, bets, and dares can often bring the response that a more serious request fails to produce. Most youngsters enjoy a little banter and can be jollied along.

4. **In-session "punishments":** Last one in does 15 bunny hops, 10 push-ups, or collects the cones can help set the standards both for the individual and the group.

5. **Severe discipline:** Drastic disciplinary measures should be used only when all else has failed. But they have to be available – in most cases as a deterrent, but occasionally for the benefit of both the team and the individual. When stern measures are called for, the soccer coach may consider the following recourse:

   a. Dropping a player from the team squad for a game or games
   b. Suspension from practice and team play
   c. Expulsion from the team club.

One hopes that such unpleasant sanctions do not become necessary, but the coach must have the authority to consider such action in the most severe of cases.

Chapter 2
ORGANISATION OF PRACTICES

What could be worse than to be the coach in charge of 20 eager young soccer players and reach a stage in the practice session when you can't think what to do next? Perhaps you've just forgotten – a temporary lapse of memory. Or maybe worse – you are genuinely at a loss as to how to progress the practice **because you were unprepared from the very start**.

1. Preparation

Preparation is the essential time taken by any thorough coach to plan the practice session in terms of:
- a. Selection of practices to work on
- b. The likely numbers of players
- c. The space available
- d. Equipment and facilities available
- e. The climate and anticipated weather conditions
- f. The physical state of the practice area.

And at the same time you must remain mindful of the young soccer players under your direction – their age and the level of their skills.

The preparation time may be as little as five minutes or as much as 50, but it **will be time well spent**.

Most coaches will be well advised to set out the session plan on paper. That is not to say that a clipboard should be the trademark of the soccer coach. While it may be a necessary piece of equipment for the coaches of other field sports to facilitate the implementation of their detailed game plans on the practice field, the *soccer* coach would, in my opinion, find it a disadvantage. Not only would it look wrong, but I believe it would inhibit his involvement. But do, by all means, carry a "memory jogger" – a small piece of paper, with an abbreviated summary of the session, in your tracksuit trouser pocket.

By setting out the session and approximating the time schedule (see Session Plan, later in the chapter), the chances of a mental block are greatly reduced; more importantly, this preparation greatly increases the likelihood of a successful practice session.

Over-preparation, as I mentioned in the introduction, can also be a problem. Moving too quickly from one practice to another in order to "follow the plan" may result in frustration for the young player – with no true practice time, and consequently no learning. Over-preparation can also be a stumbling block when the coach is faced with circumstances that he did not anticipate – a change in weather, goalposts removed that were previously there, maybe a skills practice that proves too difficult or too easy. But even in such changed circumstances, the coach may be tempted to persist with his "perfect" session. He must always be prepared to expect the unexpected – and not panic when faced with a situation that was not anticipated.

2. Facilities and equipment

In the early '70s, when I became Manager/Coach of the Third Division Club, Plymouth Argyle, I was faced with the situation of running a professional club that had no decent training facilities other than the city park adjacent to the main stadium. The parks superintendent was very co-operative and allowed us to use whatever space was available in the park – **except the soccer pitches!** Those, unfortunately but understandably, were for the exclusive use of the community clubs, for which the fields had been created.

My first major task, therefore, was to try to produce a first-rate practice environment in spite of the limitations. Very quickly we had several inexpensive portable goals designed and manufactured – two full-sized, four smaller ones. We visited the local hardware store and bought up its entire stock of broomhandles and wooden mallets. We contacted a tennis equipment manufacturer for several hundred yards of plastic tape. And we scoured Devon for every traffic cone that could be legitimately acquired!

Nature-lovers who took their morning constitutional in the park around 9.30 a.m. would see a group of soccer players emerging from the gates of the stadium carrying portable goals, sticks, cones and other paraphernalia. We then selected the best piece of grass available and started "setting up shop". The areas were spaced out, markers hammered in, goals lowered into position and the lines rolled out.

The end of the session saw a reversal of the process, with the lines carefully rolled up so that they could be easily and quickly put out the next day. Yes, there were difficulties but a "professional environment" was created.

Two years after my appointment, we completed the building of a three-field, soccer training centre, but I don't believe we suffered during our inventive practices in the park. The moral of the story? Improvisation and enthusiasm can work wonders!

Illustrations 295 and 296 show all the basic practice equipment – for a realistic outdoor session, given that there are no other markings or equipment available:

Balls: One between two is standard but they don't have to be expensive leather balls. Check the size suitability for the age group. (Item 4)

Posts (corner flags) and a mallet: In many ways it is better not to have posts with sharpened ends as this will reduce the danger should a post be struck and spin out of the ground. A mallet will drive the non-pointed poles into the ground. (Item 3)

Goals: These can be a major problem to obtain if they are not already available. Still, with some fund-raising and a little ingenuity – particularly from a father who's an engineer – lightweight, portable, collapsible goals can be constructed relatively cheaply. (Items 1 and 2)

Nets: The sight of a ball bulging the back of the net from a rocket shot is an inspiration in itself – unless you happen to be on the wrong team or the goalkeeper! For the excitement, realism and purpose that they lend to the practices, nets are worth acquiring *and* having to fix.

Identification bibs: The advantage of having opposing players in different colours cannot be emphasised too strongly. It immediately provides a contrast, and identifies the players in teams and opposite sides – the "blues" versus the "reds", for example. The uniformity of each team's colours also brings realism to the practice. (Item 5)

295

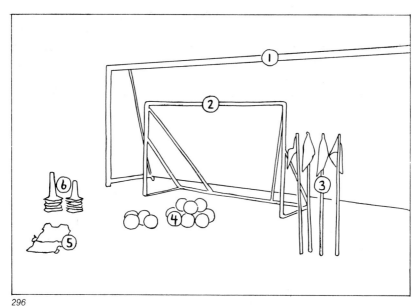

296

Cones: The standard orange traffic cone has become the universal highway symbol. It is very quickly becoming the emblem of the soccer practice field, too. A combination of larger cones (two feet) and smaller ones (one foot) is preferable, with a greater quantity of the smaller cones. A mixture of 20 – better still, 40 – will make all the difference in organising drills, and will be particularly beneficial when changing the areas as you move from one practice to another. (Item 6)

The cost, acquisition of equipment, the transportation and storage, unfortunately, may be a problem. I have made suggestions in Chapter 5 of this segment to help the coach delegate this responsibility.

3. *The use of space*

It is true luxury for a coach to have more than enough well-manicured space available – whether that be grass, artificial turf, or an indoor area. Usually space is at a premium. And the area at hand might be poorly maintained, waterlogged, or even dangerous because of potholes, grit, or glass in the soil. The coach has to assess the suitable space and maximise its usage.

The coaching grid

No one knows for certain who invented the coaching grid. Some say it originated in West Germany, others say Britain. More likely no one *invented* grids, rather, they evolved from the ingenuity and imagination of soccer-mad youngsters the world over who improvised in whatever limited space they had available.

The coaching grid, as *illustration 297* shows, is a combination of

297

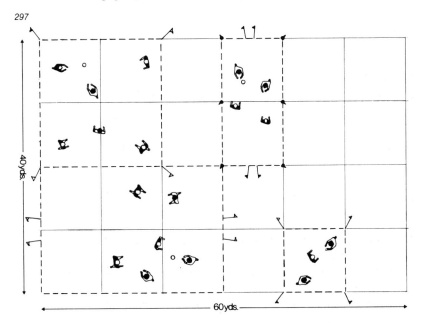

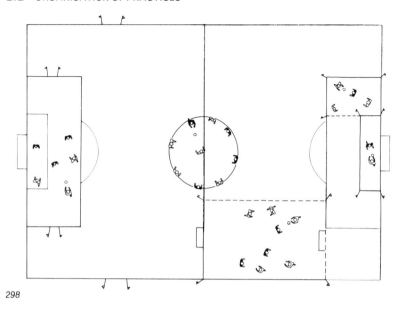

298

squares (usually 10 yards square) which can be marked into whatever space is available, and utilised for a variety of different practices and small-sided games (including, of course, those which have been discussed in Chapter 1 to 12). **There is absolutely no doubt that when you confine the practice area by clearly visible limits, the quality of the practice improves – and young players seem to prefer it.** They are regulated and have to perform under those restrictions.

The soccer field itself

The existence of a marked soccer field for the team practice is not unusual, and when available should be used fully. Look at *illustration 298* and you will appreciate how the soccer field is adapted for the team practice session.

Reality – what is it?

Reality is not having unlimited space to conduct the team practice. Reality is having a coaching grid scheme that works well in theory and an unmarked car park that your 10-year-olds have to practise on. **Reality is that in most cases, the coach will have to create his own practice areas and his own coaching grid using his own ingenuity – possibly with the co-operation of assistants** if he has any!

Illustration 299 shows a combination of field markings and portable apparatus that can produce most of the advantages of a marked-in coaching grid, thus creating very realistic practice situations.

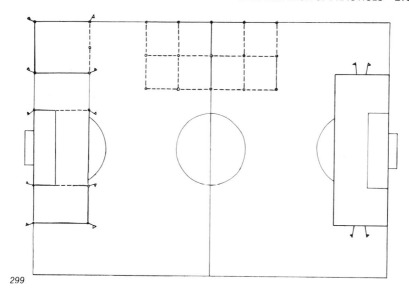

299

In *illustration 300* we see how the use of posts, cones, and portable goals – and dotted lines which represent the imagination of the young player, never to be underestimated – can create a tremendously purposeful and exciting practice situation. The coach who fires the imagination deserves much credit – but he won't need it. His reward will come from the faces and the reactions of his young charges.

Setting up and adjusting the practice area

The cardinal rule when conducting a team practice session is to arrive five minutes or so early and set out as much of the practice area as possible. This will enable players to move from one practice to another without too much of a delay. Nevertheless, no matter how much you

300

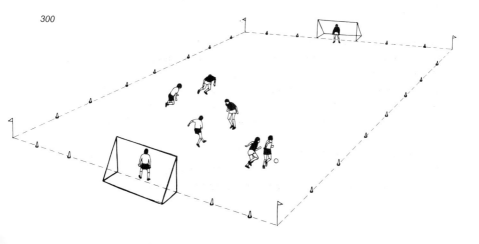

prepare or how early you arrive, there will always be distractions, and diversions and minor crises to thwart your best intentions. The secret, then, is to buy time by using drills and practices which are enjoyable, stimulating and self-administered.

Over a period of time, you will establish a repertoire of quickly-organised activities that your players know and like. These activities will leave you time to set out the playing area, ready for the next "planned" practice.

The practice area is wrong!

Planning a session on paper can turn out to be very different from actually conducting the practice out on the field. I once said to an old, experienced coach, "On paper, we should beat them easily". His tart reply was, "We're not playing on paper, we're playing on grass!" Similarly, the planned session and the estimated practice area dimensions may prove unsuitable – too big, too small, too wide, too long, or it may simply be that the players are better – or worse! – than you anticipated, an easy miscalculation to make. No matter how experienced the coach and no matter what level of play, plans will frequently go awry. The secret is not to panic. Keep cool and adjust the practice area. If necessary, rely on the fall-back position of the fun practices while making the alterations.

The "test of character" comes when having changed the practice area, it still does not work properly and there is a need for you to adjust again. Do it! You will not lose out by admitting you are wrong or by showing you are determined to get it right. On the other hand, if – in your judgement – it is not going to work at that particular session, even with adjustments, then bring in "Plan B", which can be a tried and trusted drill or small-sided game you have used a dozen times – perhaps a five versus five or seven versus seven. You may still want to revise that troublesome practice and try it out yet again at some later session. But do be realistic and remember that by a miscalculation, a practice may prove not to be feasible – a good idea just didn't work. In which case be honest enough to admit it – and abandon it!

So if the practice is not going well, be prepared to **adjust it, change it** or **suspend it**. Then **rethink it, re-present it – at a future session –** or **abandon it**!

The session plan

For the more experienced coach, setting out the session plan on paper may consist of jotting down a few short notes and time numbers. For the inexperienced coach, however, I would recommend a more formalised and detailed session plan – certainly in the initial stages of your coaching experience. There are certain basic factors that must be considered:

1. **The purpose of the session:** Moving from one practice to another, from one skill to another, may result in a mishmash of pointless activity. Try to identify the objectives of the session – perhaps long passing, or ball control or both. Don't try to cover too much in one session.

2. **Length of the session:** Estimate how long the total practice should last.

3. **Warm-up exercises or activities:** The warm-up at the start of each session is critical as it sets the standards for subsequent activities. It may be in the form of formalised stretching and running exercises or perhaps a fun series of soccer tags or relay races. Whatever the exercise, you want the players limbered up by the time it's over – ready to learn, eager to practise and play.

4. **Activity, numbers, equipment, markings and estimated time:** Include in your session plan a diagram of the practice activity; an estimate of the numbers you'll be working with and how they will be distributed (4 vs. 2 + 4 vs. 2 + 4 vs. 2 = 18); an inventory of equipment – balls, goals, cones, posts; identifying colours; and an approximate time for the successful completion of that part of the session.

5. **Concluding activity:** A major objective should be to finish every session on an up note, a high. Players should leave the practice field feeling that they have been involved in a challenging workout and have learned something about the game. They should be bubbling with the joy of success, or at least determined and enthusiastic to do better next time. To create such a positive feeling among players, I recommend that the concluding activity of the practice session always be some form of highly enjoyable game – something like a six-a-side game or three-a-side change-soccer. And it should not be an afterthought, squeezed into the last five minutes. Make it an integral part of every session, with sufficient time (15 to 30 minutes) allocated for this final activity – even to the exclusion of other "planned" activities if you find time slipping away from you.

I have included two samples to show you how sessions can be set out. They are intended merely as a guide – each coach will have a different style, using his own words, diagrams, numbers and shorthand. Initially, I have used a detailed session plan, with explanations to ensure your understanding. This is followed by an abbreviated version, one that I would use if I were preparing a session plan for my own benefit. You will see that neither plan necessitates masses of notes. It really depends on what is best for you!

If you prepare and plan, commit those plans to paper, and never lose sight of the need for flexibility, you are well on your way to running a successful and enjoyable team practice.

Session plan – example one

Purpose: Short passing and passing support

Approx. length 1 hr. 30 mins.

Numbers — 18 approx.

Age — 14-yr.-olds (boys)

Warm-up:

```
   X  X X
 X
 X   O     X       1 touch                    10 mins.
 X         X       keep ball
    X  X           (Practice 9 Page 30)
```

Stretching work at beginning — during — at end

Introduction to skills:

Games: 2 games 5 or 4-a-side

Free play for 10 mins.

Final 5 minutes — 2 touch   15 mins.

Skills work:

1.

```
XXXXX←→XXXX

XXXXX←→XXXX
```

(Practice 10 page 32)

2 touch

2 groups of 9

a. Follow pass to back of file   8 mins.

b. Turn to back of own file

2. 2 vs. 1

```
┌─────────────┐
│ X        O  │
│             │
│             │   10 yds.
│      X      │
└─────────────┘
```
(Practice 7 Page 27)

Possession

45 secs. per "Go"   10 mins.

1 identification bib per group

Groups of four (with 3's if odd numbers)
2 vs. 2 with "resting defender"

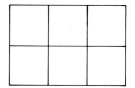

6 x 10 yd. squares

30 cones/markers

2 balls per group

3. 4 vs. 2 or 5 vs. 2 (Depending on numbers)

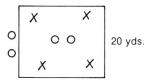

20 yds.

4A vs. 2 Def.

(2 Def. "resting")
Highest no. of
consecutive
passes

12 mins.

(Practice 12 Page 34)

Change resting defenders after 1 min.

Reverse roles attackers/defenders

Identifying bibs 4/5 per group

Reorganize cones/markers (20 yd. square)

Resting defenders retrieve balls

Competition — team with greatest consecutive pass sequence

Conclusion:

4 vs. 4 / 5 vs. 5

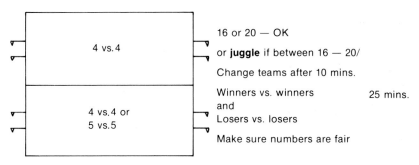

4 vs. 4

4 vs. 4 or
5 vs. 5

16 or 20 — OK

or **juggle** if between 16 — 20/

Change teams after 10 mins.

Winners vs. winners
and
Losers vs. losers

25 mins.

Make sure numbers are fair

No goalkeepers
No handling

Bibs, post, flags, portable goals?

Post-session:

Goalkeepers on own for 15 minutes

Note: Times added up (not including goalkeepers)
80 mins. — with change over etc. — 1 hr. 30 mins.

Session plan – example one

Actual – Pocket memory jogger (T.W. style)

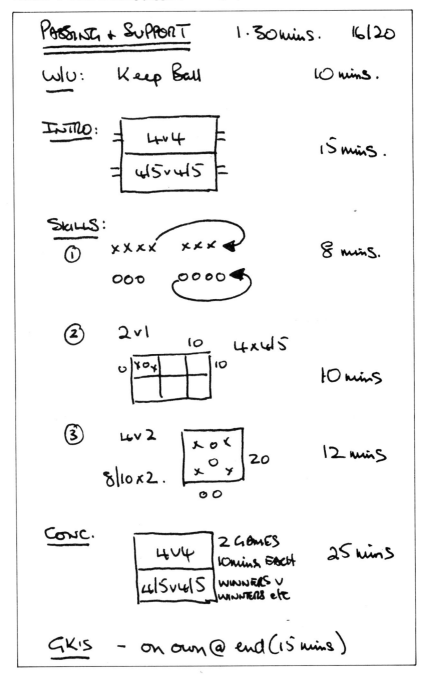

PASSING + SUPPORT   1.30mins.   16/20

W/U: Keep Ball   10 mins.

INTRO: 4v4   15 mins.
          4|5v4|5

SKILLS:
①   x x x x   x x x   8 mins.
    o o o   o o o o

②   2v1   10   4x4|5   10 mins
    o |xox| 10
       | |

③   4v2 |x o x| 20   12 mins
    8|10x2. |x o y|
              o o

CONC.   4v4   2 GAMES   25 mins
           4|5v4|5 10mins EACH
                    WINNERS v
                    WINNERS etc

GK's   - on own @ end (15 mins)

Session plan – example two

Purpose: Shooting

Approx. length — 1 hr. 20 mins.

Numbers — 14 approx.

Age — 10/11 boys

Warm-up activity:

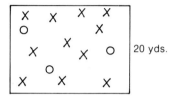

20 yds.

Soccer tag and crazy warm-up   *(See page 310)*

Hit player   10 mins.
with ball 3 players
with ball

Stretching exercises — before/during and after

1. Skills activities:

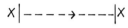

Pairs -

Driven pass
15 yds. apart
move to 25 yds.

$X|---\rightarrow \triangle ----|X$

a. "Set" targets -

Chest/thigh/left   10 mins.
foot and right
foot etc.   *(Practice 7 Page 160)*

Ball between two

Cones between two

b. Put in cone — hit

cone-driven pass
pairs — comp.   *(Practice 6 Page 49)*

2. Shooting competition:

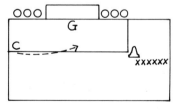

8-10 Balls

2 group (6/7 p group)   15/20 mins.

2 goalkeepers -
minimum
(Practice 6 Page 70)

Coach rolls ball across box — side foot shot

Change groups/change sides

20 shots per team per side

3. Shooting competition:

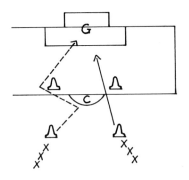

2 teams — as per (2)

Each team — in pairs

Shooter — outside of cone

Non-shooter — any run

Return back of file   15/20 mins.

Coach is server

(Practice 7 Page 72)

Conclusion:

Shooting/Change Soccer

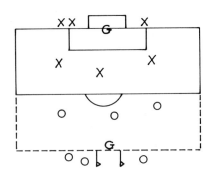

2 goalkeepers

3 vs. 3 + 3 vs. 3

(number juggling)   15/20 mins.

Change soccer principle

Coach — balls/whistle

(Practice 10 Page 75)

6 posts

6 cones

2 sets/bibs

Change ends every 5 mins.

2 points for winner — winning group declared on 3 practices

Post session: goalkeepers for 10 mins.

Total time: (excluding g.k's at end) — with change overs approx. 1 hr. 20 mins.

Session plan – example two
Actual – Pocket memory jogger (T.W. style)

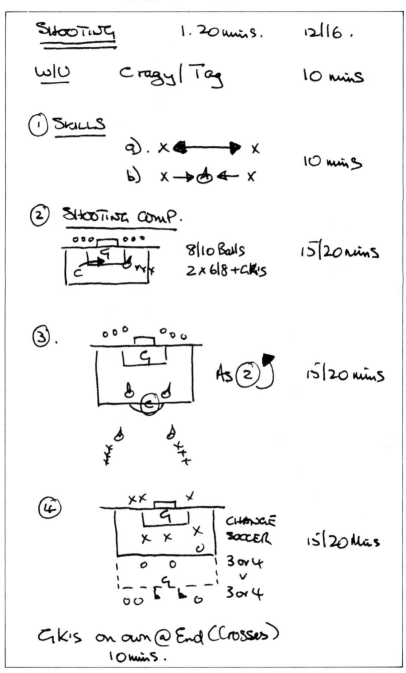

SHOOTING   1. 20 mins.   12/16.

W/U   Cragy/Tag   10 mins

① SKILLS
        a). x ⬅➡ x
                                        10 mins
        b) x ➡⬅ x

② SHOOTING COMP.
                         8/10 Balls   15/20 mins
                         2 x 6/8 + GK's

③.   As ② ↻   15/20 mins

④   CHANGE
                      SOCCER   15/20 Mins
                      3 or 4
                      v
                      3 or 4

GK's on own @ End (Crosses)
      10 mins.

Chapter 3
THE AGE OF SOCCER

Always remember that when that "bag of wind" – the leather soccer ball – begins to roll, we all become children again. The game of soccer has no age barriers, and we all tend to react in a carefree, uninhibited manner when kicking a ball around. So in that respect, participating players of seven or 70 are all looking for the same stimulation, whether it's a formal practice, a small-sided set-up, or an organised competitive game. We all enjoy playing and that should never be forgotten, certainly not by the coach! All the same, while acknowledging the similar expectations held by young and old enthusiasts, there are certain "age" considerations that a coach must be aware of when he is organising a soccer practice.

For reasons of simplicity and logic, I have grouped youngsters, by age, into three broad categories: 6 to 9 years, 9 to 14 years, and 14 to 18 years.

Before discussing specifics within the three groups, let's remember the likes and dislikes common to all young players: a desire for practices within a game format; an emphasis on playing and doing rather than listening; and a challenge within the practice in the form of a target or objective.

6 to 9 years

These boys and girls will be enthusiastic about the game and the privilege of being a member of a team. Be very aware of the following factors.

1. **Concentration:** Because the ability to absorb information and to sustain interest – for these young minds – has acute limitations, change activities frequently, always with an emphasis on enjoyment and play.

2. **Length of practice:** Because of the short concentration span and physical limitations at this age, keep practices brief – 45-60 minutes. Any longer at your peril!

3. **Technical aspect:** The fundamentals of the game need to be practised, particularly how to kick a soccer ball. Include also shooting, target and passing practices. Kicking work should be incorporated in almost every activity in as enjoyable a way as possible. For instance, shooting for goal is a good way of practising kicking as youngsters must use the right technique to strike the ball powerfully and accurately. **Ball control** should become a theme running through most sessions. Introduce **heading – but very gently and gradually**.

4. **Teamwork and understanding of the game:** I am a great advocate of six- and seven-a-side team play for youngsters in this age bracket. Such small-sided games offer a far less complex situation in which a player can more readily understand the principles of soccer. As well, with fewer players than in an 11-a-side game, each player will generally have more contact with the ball – and that in itself is beneficial. Unfortunately too many young players, parents and coaches perceive only the 11-a-side game to be "real" soccer. To convince young – and not so young – minds that all play between six and nine years of age should be something less than 11-a-side is perhaps a bit idealistic. But if I could, I would!

I would even go much further by recommending that youngsters practise in *three-a-side situations or smaller* – otherwise children will become confused by numbers, and will, in many cases, stand around wondering what is expected of them. The chances are, and I don't mean this unkindly, that the coach will be no less confused, particularly when called upon to sort out these complications. So stick to two versus two's, three versus three's, and leave the five versus five's and six versus six's to the final game – if, in fact, you feel you need to increase numbers as the finale to the team practice. Should you want confirmation of the desirability of small numbers, just observe youngsters in this age bracket. You can bet good money that they "pal around" in two's and three's and rarely in larger groups. The "gang"comes later.

Fitness work

You needn't concern yourself with additional fitness workouts for youngsters at this stage in their development. Their participation in the practices and games will be more than sufficient.

Positional play

Unfortunately, the coach is too often pressured into believing that positional play needs careful attention at this age – mainly because of the 11-a-side match requirements. It is another very good reason why 11-a-side soccer is a hindrance rather than a help to the development of very young soccer players. Six- to-nine-year-olds should have no set positions. Each youngster should be practising to become an all-round soccer player, adept in all skills and therefore all positions. No player should be "condemned" to the goalkeeping role at eight years of age. Nor should a player be categorised as a defender or a midfielder too early in his soccer career.

The coach is advised to concentrate his efforts on all the fundamental skills and aspects of the game that are outlined in chapters 1 to 12, particularly those suggestions in Section I of each chapter.

Summary

A coach of six- to nine-year-olds should emphasise the basics of the game – passing, controlling the ball, shooting for goal, heading the ball *without* opposition, crossing from the flanks, basic goalkeeping – but most of all, *kicking* a soccer ball. Keep the practice sessions relatively short – 45 minutes to an hour – and spend at least half the time in free play, i.e. small-sided games with few restrictions other than the fundamental rules. Change the activity periodically, and make sure it is enjoyable. Introducing a competitive aspect to the practices is not as important as it is for 10- to 18-year-olds. Keep team games down in size to three-a-side or smaller. Finally, use every gimmick in the book – sweets, push-ups, prizes – and stock up on headache pills for personal use!

9 to 14 years

At this age a youngster is a little more mature and becoming aware of the need for co-operation in order to meet team objectives. He is more "group conscious", and therefore is not only capable of performing in group practices but in many ways is happier to be in those particular circumstances. Section II of Chapters 1 to 12 outlines the type of practices that a parent or coach can help organise for a small group, and it is in this area that the team coach should concentrate his efforts, by incorporating those exercises into the team practice.

Opposition

The player in this age bracket is becoming very aware of the need to overcome the opposition, and that factor of the game now becomes an important consideration. Consequently, there should be a greater emphasis on opposed practices such as the two versus one, the two versus two and the three versus two.

Numbers

Even though there is an awakening of group consciousness at this age, the numbers should still be kept relatively small and "understandable" – two versus one, up to four versus four, with any permutation in between. These youngsters still tend to view the opposition in terms of a one on one, "match-up" type situation, even within a four versus four practice. The coach should be aware of this, and incline the players towards the team unit concept – but not too rapidly. One versus one thinking can be changed by the use of three versus three's and four versus four's where the players are encouraged to combine as a small team and are praised when they do. Apart from the competitive games, I would still respectfully suggest that 11-a-side circumstances be avoided as much as possible in the team practice session. There is still much basic development to be accomplished at this age.

Fitness

As youngsters approach their teens, they become more aware of their bodies and their physique. Boys start concerning themselves with their "manliness", and see racing, shows of strength and endurance running as tests. Be very careful that this does not assume too great an importance in the team practice although, quite obviously, it should become a consideration. The prime concern should be to continue their skills development. Fitness in this age bracket becomes a more serious aspect of the game, but priorities must be kept in mind. Running over every inch of the field for 90 minutes is a remarkable achievement, but if the player lacks the skills ability to do something positive in the areas he's charging about in, he will contribute little to the team or the game.

Concentration

Most, if not all, of these youngsters will have been involved in organised soccer for at least two or three years, so both their desire to learn and their ability to assimilate information is greater. Just the extra years help enormously. Their concentration span is, of course greater than that of the younger players. Still, you must never lose sight of the need for action, the eagerness to do, the desire to play. Don't bore the shorts off them!

Positional play

The need to be in the right place at the right time is becoming more apparent to these players, and therefore more important. At this age, they will be ready for some practice in the different positions on the team. Even so, be cautious and don't commit a player to a particular position. Many things can happen, and probably will, between the ages of 14 and 18. As an example, I saw the greatest 13-year-old goalkeeper ever – in my opinion – fail to make the professional ranks. Not because of any lack of ability, but simply because he failed to grow any taller after the age of 14. So let players experiment and gain an appreciation of all roles on the team. Position them as defenders, midfielders, and attackers and goalkeepers rather than as fullbacks, wingers and central defenders. Encourage goalkeepers to have an alternative outfield position.

Length of session

Nothing can kill players' enthusiasm like an overlong session. A practice lasting 1¼ hours should be ample; 90 minutes is often too much. A team practice should be like reading a good book – when it's ended, you know it's ended, but you wish it hadn't.

Summary

Players between 10 and 14 remain very much in the development stage, so practice in the fundamentals of the game is called for. Passing, control, shooting, heading – these should still form the substantial "learning" part of the session – both with and without opposition included in the practice. "If you can't pass, you can't play", so there is no point in trying to progress the players if they are not proficient in the basics.

Some aspect of fitness work should be introduced but it should not be too scientific or intense. In skills work, keep the numbers relatively small and therefore "understandable" to the players. Deal with positional play in fairly general terms, but make certain *the practices are for all players*, on the understanding that the players can and will change their positional preference as the years go by. Above all, have them spend the bulk of the practice session playing the game in one form or another.

14 to 18 years

These are young men and women, and not adults. But they are maturing quickly and becoming aware of what it means to be a grown-up. That is one very good reason why they enjoy soccer so much – it enables them to temporarily put out of their minds the sometimes daunting prospect of adult responsibility! Seriously, it is natural for teenagers to be anxious about what lies just up the road, but this does affect their behaviour and must be taken into account.

In terms of soccer, while they see themselves as individuals in their own right, they want to be, and appreciate the privilege of being, part of a team. And to satisfy their own egos and build confidence, *they want to be a significant part*. The team practice must take this into consideration, and be oriented towards team play and the role of the individual within the team. It is only with this age group that the coach should encourage each player to evaluate his particular strengths and weaknesses and decide where his talents can best be utilised on the team. But – and yes, you've read my mind – avoid condemning a player to a position once and for all. Keep encouraging them and giving them practice in all the skills of the game, so they can continue to develop as all-round players who may well change their position next week or next season!

Fitness

Fitness now becomes a critical part of the team practice. Most players, at this stage in their development, have got the message: soccer is a running game, and those who run fastest and longest can be valuable team members (provided they can do something with the ball once they get it!). Moreover, the challenge to be strong and fit is a powerful motivator.

Length of session

Again, 90 minutes is ample. If the session is organised properly, the player should be "pleasantly fatigued" by the time it's over – particularly if the final part is reserved for 10 to 15 minutes of fitness work, which should consist mostly of sprinting and running. You will find, with this age group, that the final segment of fitness work is, most times, a very acceptable way of completing the team session. This should not be misconstrued as contradictory to an earlier recommendation to finish with the game. Have the game as the culmination of the ball work, then present the fitness segment as the final challenge. The players will moan and groan – but they will love it. Not that they will ever admit it to you!

If a practice has been particularly interesting, players can probably sustain a two-hour session, but I would advise against it. In 90 per cent of cases, coaches are sure to achieve *more* in 1½ hours than in two – that final half-hour can easily become counterproductive.

Technical development

Continue to work on the basics – heading, passing, shooting, crossing, control – both without opposition, and in opposed practices such as one versus one, two versus one and two versus two. Relate the practices to the parts of the field where they actually happen, and so make meaningful the roles of the players within the practice from a positional point of view. For example, a two versus one situation going into the penalty area. Or a two versus two on the edge of the penalty area, looking to get a strike at goal, using two strikers versus two defenders, plus a goalkeeper. These are basic practices for players but in specific positions on the field of play.

Team understanding

I said in the introduction to this segment that 14- to 18-year-olds are more team conscious and mindful of their role in the team, and that this should be reflected in the type of practice you set up. For instance, practise in units, such as a defensive back four, or a front three (illustrated in Practice 7, Chapter 11 and Practice 6, Chapter 12).

Don't be concerned if you are a coach with limited experience. You don't have to be too ambitious in the team practice, nor gamble with your limited knowledge and experience. A lively session incorporating the suggestions given in this book, and using the practice considerations provided in the earlier part of Chapters 1 to 12 will be fine.

If you want to progress yourself in terms of advanced soccer coaching techniques, inquire about possible soccer certification programmes. Information on these should be available from your national or local soccer association.

Summary

Although there has been a greater emphasis on team and positional play with this age group, the sessions should still remain very similar in content to those for the two younger groups. Fundamental and fun practices, as always, are the order of the day, as is the playing of the game. Don't make the mistake of thinking these young men and women have suddenly become solemn, task-oriented robots. They are still very much in the development stage, and it would be wrong to consider them mature players. Don't accept certain limitations in their play with a shrug of the shoulders, but continue trying to help them develop their soccer skills. In other words, treat them like adults while remembering they are kids at heart. Aren't we all?

Conclusions

The three age groups of young soccer players – 6 to 9 years, 9 to 14 years, and 14 to 18 years – can be almost directly related to the format of Chapters 1 to 12 in the technical section of this book. Section I concentrates on the basic techniques and the mastering of those techniques; Section II is mostly concerned with the application of those techniques in a small group-type situation, still related very much to the game; Section III is the team consideration. That, in my opinion, should be your approach to the organisation and conducting of the team practice for the three age groups. But remember that we're only talking about tendencies and not ironclad directives. The sessions for all three groups should have remarkable similarities. A casual observer happening by the soccer field should see a group of young people enjoying *playing* the game of soccer.

Chapter 4
THE SEASON'S PLAN

Several years ago, I was asked to address the professional soccer coaches of England on the subject of a season's plan. Before the lecture, one old coach remarked somewhat cynically, "There's no way you can plan for a season. It all depends on results".

Employed as he was in the cut-throat business of professional sport, he had a valid point.

However, I asked him what he would do if he had to make his way that very day to the city of Penzance in Cornwall. We were in the Midlands at the time, and Penzance was approximately 300 miles to the southwest of us. "Well," he said, and thought for a while, "I'd buy a map first of all and work out the best way to get there". "And then what?" I asked. "Well, I'd weigh up the best method of getting there – by car or by train. A lot would depend on how soon I had to be there". Anyway, he got the point. We both agreed that on the soccer journey, you need to know where you intend to go and how you are going to get there. But you also need to be prepared for the unexpected obstacles and diversions that might necessitate a change of plan along the way. The cantankerous but successful coach later confessed to me that he had always set out a season's plan each year anyway!

So in the development programme over a soccer season, there should be clear objectives and a plan to help achieve those objectives. The plan should need to be altered only if a more attractive direction later presents itself or problems along the way require a review.

Without the master plan, the coach lives from one week to the next – or even worse, from one game to the next. Each team practice runs the risk, therefore, of becoming a hodgepodge of assorted skills and activities or else the same boring session repeated weekly.

The master plan does not have to be a sophisticated, 30-page document but rather like a travel itinerary – a one-page outline containing the critical and relevant details.

In formulating a season's plan, there are certain key factors that must be considered:

Critical time periods

1. Start of the season
2. Christmas, Easter, the summer break
3. Exchanges and tours
4. Tournaments
5. Play-offs
6. Roster deadlines
7. Drafts
8. School commitments, such as exams

Climate

Are there seasonal peculiarities to be kept in mind, such as very wet winters, reduced daylight in autumn and winter, excessive cold or heat?

Facilities

Do you need to alter the practice and playing facilities during the season – outdoor to indoor, grass to artificial? Will alterations affect the season's plan?

Basic skills development

Certain basic skills (those outlined in Chapters 1 to 9) need to be developed rain or shine, indoors or outdoors, win or lose. They should be included in almost every session and therefore built into the season's plan.

Team understanding and practical considerations

"Chalk talk" has become almost an institution in the locker rooms of North American sports. But fundamental understanding of team tactical requirements (Chapters 10 to 12) needs the proper practical inclusion in the season's programme – no one ever scored an authentic goal on a blackboard. So team understanding, as well as set plays such as corner kicks, free kicks, throw-ins, even penalties, should be an integral part of the plan.

Blocks of practice

The "block method" is a system whereby the team concentrates on one particular aspect of the game for an extended period of time – perhaps four to six weeks. Heading is a fine example of a skill that merits such block treatment, especially since it is easily neglected in the absence of a planned concentration. This doesn't mean that during the block period everything else is ignored. It simply means that there is an obvious *emphasis* on a specific skill during that period of time, and that a significant part of each session is devoted to its understanding.

Flexibility

It can't be said often enough – that every coach must be sensitive to fast-changing circumstances and unexpected occurrences. No coach can ever map out an exact plan – whether that's a game plan, a session plan, or a season's plan. Every soccer plan, like every coach, has to be adaptable – or maybe has to be changed completely. Coaches get changed too, you know! But, of course, a plan has the great benefit of making people question the need for change. Individuals who advocate change simply for its own sake often worsen rather than improve a situation. To help you visualise the format we've been discussing, here is a simple one-page season's plan you can use as a model.

Season's plan

For a 9-year-old boys' team

Aug. 15	Final registration date
Sept. 1	Start of Pre-Season and Exhibition Schedule
Sept. 14	Start of regular season
Oct. 17	End of daylight savings time
Oct. 21	Indoor training commences
Nov. 3	Exchange
Dec. 14	End of first half of the season
Jan. 14	Start of second half of the season
Feb. 9	Exchange
March 1	Sufficient daylight to recommence outdoor practice
April 15	End of regular schedule
April 22	Play-off Tournament/End of season

Priorities for team practice

1. Basic passing skills

2. Ball control practice

3. Shooting practice

4. Attacking support (2 & 3's)

5. Defensive support (2 & 3's)

6. Appreciation of width

7. Basic heading practice

8. Tactical practice

    a. Attacking corners
    b. Throw-ins

Block work

Heading block
March 1 to April 15 (outdoor)

Shooting block
Aug. 23 to Oct. 21 (outdoor)

Priority 8 to be emphasised early/late season (outdoor)

Goalkeeping

Goalkeeping "concentration" outdoor periods (autumn/spring) – particularly crosses/through-balls, distribution

Shot stopping work – indoor (with agility mats)

It would be very easy to jot down 20 priorities. But it would be wrong. This is one season's plan, and even having eight priorities is perhaps overly ambitious.

Chapter 5
HELP! I'M ONLY THE COACH

However you came about the job of coach – whether you were asked, browbeaten, volunteered or even tricked – the fact remains that you are a person prepared to take on responsibility. But where does that responsibility begin and end?

Your leadership abilities, your attention to detail, your concern that all goes well – these sterling attributes will inevitably mean that others will leave you to do it all, unless you remind them, politely of course, that they also have responsibilities to assume.

There are two main groups of people associated with youth soccer, apart from the coaches and administrators. They are the players themselves and their parents. Both groups should be organised in different ways to allow the coach to concentrate on the difficult and demanding task of coaching the team.

There are a host of related matters to keep track of, and what follows is a check-list that can be attended to by "someone". The plain truth is that it may still fall on the coach's shoulders to delegate the responsibilities. He has every right to expect co-operation, but may well have to use his coaching or, in this case, his coaxing experience to bring forth that help.

Most youth teams I have known have normally established an efficient "off the field team" very quickly. Usually there is a manager to work with the coach – a husband and wife combination is not uncommon. But the considerations, particularly in today's world, are so many that a "working committee" may be a better way of sharing the load. This committee, of course, works alongside the manager and coach.

It shouldn't need to be too formal an arrangement *but* a clarification of responsibilities acceptable to all concerned is essential. For instance, in the event – heaven forbid – of a mishap, has insurance been looked after? It's no good afterwards saying, "I thought it was Joan Brown's job. I seem to recall we said something about it last September". Certain situations must be properly planned for.

The check-list should provide useful guidelines for day to day running of a youth soccer team.

Registrations

Who fills out the forms?
Who collects them and sends off the money?
Who finalises the roster?
Who arranges a transfer of registration?
Who sends in the team sheets, results, etc?
Who arranges the schedule?

Facilities

Who is responsible for booking the game and practice fields?
Do you need indoor facilities for team practice?
Who pays for the facilities?
Do you have locker rooms with showers?
Who is responsible for looking after them and their security?

Uniforms

What is the club policy regarding uniforms?
Who supplies them?
Who pays for them?
Who looks after them on a game-by-game basis and at the end of the season?
How is a lost uniform replaced?
Do you have, or need to have, a team tracksuit?

Practice and coaching apparatus

How many cones, balls, bibs, posts and goals do you need?
Who supplies them?
Who looks after them?
Where does the money for purchase come from?

Weekly information

Who informs the players, the coaches, the committee and the parents of any changes or new events?
Is it the coach, the manager or the secretary?
Is it done by phone or letter?

Transportation

How do you travel to "away" games?
Do you rely on parents for transportation?
Who organises the travel plans?
Who drives?
Does it require any special insurance?

Medical arrangements

Does the team have an official trainer?
Is the coach or manager qualified to administer first aid?
Do you always check the nearest phone location and hospital number, and carry a ten pence piece – in case of an emergency?
Do you carry a first aid kit?
Are you and the club insured?

Referees

Do they need to be notified of upcoming games, particularly rearranged games?
Is it the responsibility of the club or the soccer association?
Who pays the referee – and linesmen, if appointed – their fees and expenses?
Is the team responsible for providing linesmen?

Fund raising

With expenses such as uniforms, facilities, equipment (balls, posts, cones, etc.), tours, exchanges:
Who is responsible for fund raising?
Is there a committee?
Are the players expected to be involved in fund raising?

Game organisation

Who looks after the opening of the locker room?
Who locks up the locker room?
Who supplies refreshments at half time and after the game?
Does anybody look after the needs of the referee?
Are linesmen supplied by the home team?
Do you require any insurance for theft?
Who supplies the balls, linesman flags, corner posts, nets – even goals?

Insurance

It is necessary to arrange coverage for:

1. The regular games?
2. Travel to "away" games?
3. Medical expenses if on tour or on an exchange outside the country?
4. Other contingencies such as theft?

The media

Should the local media be informed of results and other details?
Do you need a separate person to handle public relations?

Tours and exchanges

This is a major responsibility if embarked upon.
Should the team go on tour or arrange an exchange?
Who is to be responsible for the organisation?

Does it require a committee?
How is the funding to be organised?
Are there any special requirements – passports, identification, medical certificates, etc.?

Every club no doubt will have additions and deletions to make, depending on its own requirements for the smooth running of the team. But do set these out on paper to avoid any important omissions or misunderstandings.

The players and even "absent parents" should pitch in and share some responsibility. Laundering, the provision of refreshments on a rotating basis, fund raising, the donation of equipment – all are duties that can, and should, be delegated to parents and their children. The coach is not a babysitter and should insist that parents make their proper contribution.

Don't be afraid of asserting yourself. It is perfectly fair for you to expect everyone who is in some way involved with the team to assume part of the responsibility. **The fact is that you, the coach will *still* end up doing more than anyone else! But then this is the world's greatest game – win, lose or tie!**

Note

It is recommended that shinguards be worn by players at all times, during both match play and practice. Shinguards are not uncomfortable to wear and provide considerable protection from injuries, even fractures.

FIFA, the game's world governing body, has now made the wearing of shinguards compulsory in all of its tournaments and competitions. Most domestic leagues and National Associations have followed this lead and enforced similar rulings of their own.

THE GAMES SOCCER PLAYERS PLAY

The game of soccer is recognised as the world's leading team game. It is played on regulation-sized fields, 11 players per team, in accordance with strict rules.

Every soccer practice should be as close as possible to the real thing while at the same time emphasising a particular skill or aspect of the game. Wherever feasible, a practice should be presented in an enjoyable game format which challenges the competitive nature of players – even though the practice may be only one versus one. Of course, occasionally it is desirable to reduce the competitive element so that learning can take place in a more relaxed situation, but generally speaking, the format will add to the realism of the practice.

The 11-a-side game is seldom used in practice sessions. It is too complex, and with only one ball among 22, does not give the individual sufficient opportunity for practice. Most games should be scaled down in terms of numbers and space for practice purposes – two versus one, four versus two, five versus five.

Some clarification, along with additional examples of the types of games soccer players play in the practice sessions, will be beneficial.

Conditioned games

A conditioned game can be any small-sided game – two versus two, four versus two, five versus five – even 11-a-side, for that matter – in which an extra "condition", or unofficial rule, is imposed. The condition is meant to focus attention on a particular part of the game.

For example, in a two-touch situation, the extra rule stipulates that a player is permitted only up to two touches of the ball before it must go to another player. Failure to keep the condition – more than two touches, in this case – results in a free kick to the opposition. The idea of two-touch is to improve the ball control – the first touch – and to make youngsters more aware of supporting players. Passing is improved as players must be aware – even before controlling the ball – of what they are going to do with it on the second touch, and then usually they pass the ball to a team mate. In some cases, the best thing to do on the second touch is to shoot or clear the ball out of the defensive area, or perhaps cross the ball in front of the goal.

Players will often resist conditioned games because they find them too restrictive and frustrating. But they are valuable learning tools. The general rule to follow with conditions in practice sessions is "little but often". Impose the rule, withdraw, give them free play, then impose the condition again. In the final analysis, *you will* have to decide what is in the players' best interests and structure your session accordingly.

It is a good idea to finish most practice sessions with a game – seven-a-side, five-a-side, whatever the numbers permit. If you have allowed 15 to 20 minutes for the final small-sided game, don't be afraid of placing a condition on the game for the first five to seven minutes, then making the balance of the time free play.

The following is a list of conditions you may find useful, and an explanation of what the additional rule will emphasise. There are many others besides those presented here and the coach is always free to devise some of his own.

Two-touch

As previously described, this is probably the most often used condition in the soccer world. Start younger players off with three-touch maximum, as two-touch may be too difficult.

Two-touch:

1. Emphasises the value of good considerate passing. A good pass helps the team mate receiving the ball who is also restricted to two-touches.
2. Encourages sharp controlling of the ball in order to set up the correct position for the pass – the second touch.
3. Encourages team mates to take up good positions (supporting play) in order to make it easier for the man on-the-ball.
4. Aids players in developing an awareness of their team mates and opponents, as they do not have the alternative of holding on to the ball. Therefore, they must look around and assess the situation at all times – even when not in possession.

One-touch

An extremely difficult condition and one that should not be attempted until players are very comfortable with two-touch. Excellent condition for:

1. Making players think and plan what they are going to do with the ball before it arrives.

2. Encouraging good passing so as to assist the person receiving the ball who also has only one-touch. The accuracy and speed of the pass becomes very important.

3. Encouraging players to support the team mate receiving the ball, as that player has only one-touch and needs all the help he can get.

Head-a-goal

This condition rules that goals can only be scored using the head. It is particularly effective when authentic full-sized goals are available and players are sufficiently skilled at heading to avoid clumsy aerial challenges, as these may easily result in head injuries. Be extremely cautious regarding the use of this condition with young children. Head-a-goal emphasises:

1. Realistic attacking and defensive heading. It may be worth dispensing with goalkeepers to encourage even more heading in the penalty/goal areas.

2. Crossing of the ball, if a reasonably wide practice area is available. This will be the most effective method of producing scoring chances from headers.

Pass and move

This simple condition compels the player who passes the ball to move into a new position. (Too often, after players pass the ball, they stand and admire their handiwork or worse, throw up their arms in disgust because their own pass was poor or perhaps the receiving player failed to react properly.) "Pass and Move" introduces an important aspect of the game, particularly to young players.

It disciplines the player to take a new position, having released the ball. It can be made even more effective by awarding a free kick to the opposition when a player fails to move after a pass, and maybe imposing a further punishment of 10 push-ups to the offending player.

Pass and support, or follow-your-pass

This condition is almost identical to the previous one except that the player making a pass is now conditioned to follow it, and so supports his own pass – often a necessary part of the team play.

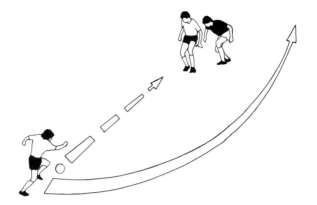

301

Pass and overlap

A further development of the previous conditions is where the young-ster playing the ball must follow his pass, and attempt to go around his team mate receiving the ball and into an advanced position (see *illustration 301*). This emphasises movement but in addition, intro-duces the "overlap run", which encourages players to think more posi-tively about getting forward, and making runs in advance of the ball.

Must beat opponent before passing

The condition here insists that a player cannot pass the ball until he dribbles past an opponent. This is an extremely artificial condition and should be used sparingly, but it does present the opportunity for tack-ling and encourages the valuable skill of dribbling.

Right foot or left foot only

With this condition, players are permitted to use only one foot – either the left or right. As most soccer players are more comfortable using their right foot, "left foot only" is probably more beneficial. Apart from the obvious advantages of practising with the non-dominant foot, there can be more psychological gains as players who normally avoid their less comfortable foot discover that perhaps they are not as weak as they thought they were. This may well encourage them to practise more often with the non-dominant foot in future.

Special games for soccer

There are games other than conditioned ones that have been designed especially to highlight specific aspects of the game. These may also be conditioned if you so choose. The following are some you may find useful in practice sessions.

The man-marking game

In this game, even numbers are selected – four versus four or five versus five, for example – and an appropriate size field set out with a marked half-way line (see *illustration 302*).

Small goals can be used with no goalkeepers, or full-sized goals (portable if available) with goalkeepers. Each player is assigned an opponent to man-mark except for two free defenders ("sweepers"), one on each team. The free players are limited to their defensive half of the field, and to two touches. The rest of the players, paired off as they are, can only tackle their assigned opponent. The free defender inevitably becomes the last line of defence and is allowed to tackle anybody. All players are allowed to intercept passes but can only tackle their assigned opponent, the punishment being a free kick or, within a certain area close to goal, a penalty.

The free players are changed frequently so that the two become a marking pair, while another pair takes their turn in becoming the free defenders. The man-marking game emphasises:

1. The discipline of good marking.
2. An awareness of opponents, position, and the necessity to recover onto your opponent when possession is lost.

302

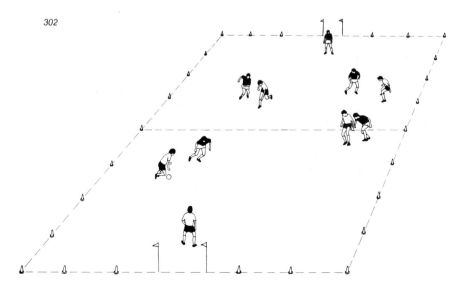

3. The attacking play of losing your marker to steal forward into an attacking position.

4. The excellent practice for the free defenders or sweepers in taking up essential defending, covering and supporting positions.

The game is very much one of cat-and-mouse, and there is a certain amount of gambling involved. For instance, if a player attempts to steal into a good attacking position on the blind side of his marker, and the move breaks down, he may find himself at a disadvantage, unable to recover quickly enough to prevent his opponent from having a relatively free run at goal. The coach must recognise what each player is attempting to do, and not criticise a player who has made a positive forward run just because he is unable to get back in time. However, every player *is* required to attempt to recover back when possession is lost as the free defender may be able to buy time for recovery. This is a great game that requires discipline and hard work but it's good fun. Highly recommended.

Four goals game

In the four goals game, each team attacks two goals and defends two goals (see *illustration 303*). This game needs careful introduction as initially, it can be confusing to young players, but once they get the idea

303

they will enjoy it and have no problem understanding the requirements.
The game emphasises:

1. Switching play, when one goal is so well defended that it becomes
more profitable to try to attack goal two.

2. The importance of being aware of every opponent, particularly when
the opposition has the ball. It forces players to look around constantly
to assess the situation. Just one player escaping attention can sneak in
unnoticed by the opposition, receive a pass and score in the goal that
seemed least threatened.

Four goals-non-stop soccer

In this game, four goals (cones or posts) are set one yard apart,
approximately five yards in from each corner. An appropriate size area
is marked out according to the numbers and ages of players (see
illustration 304). For example, 14-year-olds playing seven versus seven
would be fine in a 50-yard square. For a five versus five game involving
9-year-olds, a 30-yard square would be more appropriate. The object is
to score goals by playing through the front of the goals, but possession
can be maintained after scoring. If the ball goes out of play, the game is
resumed by a conventional throw-in.

The rules can be quite complicated, and it requires total concentration (perhaps a degree in mathematics!) to maintain control and keep
score but here goes:

1. One goal (point) can be scored by playing the ball through the front
of any goal (no goal from the back).

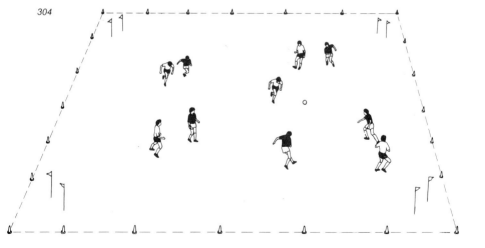

304

2. Alternatively, a goal (a point) can be scored by keeping a sequence of passes going (say five) without the opposition intercepting or the ball going out of play.

3. A goal can be scored in the middle of a sequence of passing by playing the ball through the front of one of the goals while the team maintains possession. Then a further point is scored if five passes are achieved.

4. Once a point is scored by five consecutive passes – as long as possession is maintained – the sequence starts again.

You can keep score using a tennis type system where "sets" are played, the winner being the team that scores six points. After a short break the second set commences, and so on. Three sets in a game of this nature can last anywhere from 10 to 25 minutes.

The game is all action – great fun but trying, at times, for the coach. It does produce some excellent practice situations, though.

a. Players in possession need to decide if they will go for goal or merely keep possession while awaiting the goal-scoring opportunity.

b. Players are encouraged to look around and switch the point of attack as one goal becomes tightly defended.

c. The team not in possession cannot just mark the goals, as the opposition will build up passes and score anyway. The non-possession team must work energetically, and as a team, to get the ball back as soon as possible.

d. Players who are preoccupied with scoring through the goals will make it easier for the opposition. On the other hand, players who indulge in a series of short passes without looking to switch the play will quickly lose sight of the total field and players, draw in the opposition, and consequently lose the ball more readily.

Introducing the game is not easy but it can be achieved in stages. For instance:

1. At first don't introduce the condition that five consecutive passes score a point or goal. Let the play proceed allowing scoring in any of the four goals.

2. Sooner or later, the "penny will drop" and the team not having possession will assign one player to each of the four goals to stand in front of it and make it impossible to score. It is at this stage that you introduce the further rule that five consecutive passes score a goal. The group will see why it is necessary, and will understand what then has to be done to score or to prevent goals or points.

Throw-head-catch

This is a fine game for working on opposed heading situations. Again, a word of caution, as challenging for the ball in the air involves the risk of injury. Players should be fairly accomplished, and should have been given ample practice in the heading progressions – from the basics to controlled opposed heading practices (see Chapter 5).

Using a field of adequate size, goals are set up at each end. The coach can decide whether to use goalkeepers although with small goals, it is often better not to. Throw-head-catch is played in the following manner:

1. It is started by a player having the ball in his hand.
2. No player is allowed to move with the ball in his hand.
3. The sequence runs as follows: the player with the ball throws it to the head of a team mate, who heads the ball either back to the initial thrower or on to another team mate.
4. Progress is made down the field by the throw and the headed pass.
5. Ultimately, the ball has to be thrown into the scoring area and a goal can be scored only by the head.
6. If after a throw the ball is not headed by anyone, possession is then conceded to the opposition.
7. Otherwise, at all times, the throw-head-catch sequence must be adhered to and the opposition competes on the same basis – that is, they can challenge for the header, or they can try to intercept and catch after the header.
8. Whenever the ball goes out of play or a goal is scored, the game is restarted by a throw from the place where the ball left the field.

Finding the goalkeeper

This game has one unusual feature: each team's goalkeeper plays at the wrong end of the field.

As you can see in *illustration 305*, there are no goals, merely a zone to which the goalkeepers are restricted. The zone is out of bounds to the outfield players. The object is for each team to chip the ball into the hands of their own keeper, who must catch the ball without leaving his zone for a goal to be scored. After a goal is scored, play is restarted by the goalkeeper placing the ball on the edge of his zone for one of the opposition to commence the play. This game, besides being enjoyable, brings out two very important aspects of soccer:

1. It forces youngsters to play very accurate floated passes forward to the goalkeeper. This is an effective forward ball in the 11-a-side game.

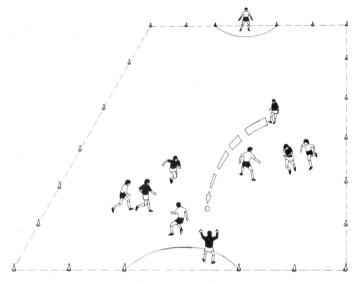

305

2. From the defensive point of view it compels the team to close down the opposition in order to prevent the possibility of balls being chipped forward to the target (goalkeeper). Every time a goal is scored, there has to be some faulty defensive play, as well as good attacking. It should be obvious to the coach and the players that to reduce the possibility of goals being scored, it will be necessary to hustle the opposition when it has possession (see Chapter 7 on hustling and Chapter 11 on defensive support).

Other games for the team practice
Crazy warm-up

The "crazy warm-up" is my own invention – an amalgamation of different drills and games which I have pulled together over a period of time. The warm-up has found ready acceptance among players of all ages and skills, from six-year-olds to top flight professionals.

The players are confined to an area approximately 20 yards square (see *illustration 306*). No player is allowed to leave the area. The exact requirements and methods will vary according to the circumstances and the number of players.

It is strongly recommended that with older players, you allow a period of time (30 to 60 seconds) for stretching exercises between each game change – especially if the games are being used as a warm-up before the major part of the team practice.

306

The following games make up the crazy warm-up:

1. Three players from the group are each given a ball. *No handling* is allowed to start with. Initially, no one is allowed to run – only walk. The players with a ball can rid themselves of it only by hitting another player who hasn't a ball with an aimed pass. After several minutes and some stretching work, allow everyone to begin running within the game rules.
2. The next change allows the three players in possession of balls to pick them up. They can then tag any other player by hitting him on any part of the body with the ball. The players without a ball need to be very alert, always looking around and prepared to move quickly to take avoiding action. The tagging can be made more specific by the coach ruling that "you must hit the lower legs only, but players can protect their legs with their arms and hands, or backsides and the back only". Needless to say, there is fun and skulduggery aplenty as players with the ball can hide it behind their backs and surprise the less observant.
3. The crazy warm-up can then be developed into a normal type of tag by touching another with the hand within the area. One person is selected to be "it" and must touch another player to get himself "off". The difference here, though, is that any player holding one of the three soccer balls used in the previous part of the crazy warm-up cannot be tagged. The skill and fun are just beginning as those three players with the ball should follow around the player who is "it" and be prepared to throw the ball to a colleague in distress.

By skilful transfer of the balls, it can be made very difficult for the player who is "it" to get himself "off". However, the coach must make sure that a player with a ball doesn't merely stand around and use it to protect himself and have a rest. If this is happening, the coach should stop the practice and make the lazy ballholder "it". Once the group becomes adept at using three balls, be prepared to reduce it to two or, if necessary, one. Normally two to three balls is the right number. The coach should take care that time doesn't run away, as the crazy warm-up often stretches into a half-hour or 40 minute session. Keep an eye on the watch and see to it that the stretching work is attended to between changes.

Relays

The final segment of "The Games Soccer Players Play" deals with relay racing. A variety of relays – with or without a soccer ball – can be used, even *devised* by the coach. Relay racing as an activity has much to recommend it: it is generally easy to organise; very effective when space is limited (in an indoor gymnasium for example); aids team discipline as players have to work together in order to win; and is always enthusiastically and competitively accepted by youngsters.

1. Sprint relay

On the starting signal, the first players sprint forward around cones positioned 10 or 15 yards away, back and around the back cone before touching the second person. To stop any cheating, each runner can be asked to carry a baton or a training bib – anything to pass over once the player has come round the back cone. For meaningful participation, teams of three or four are better than larger groups of seven or eight. Cheaters are always punished by imposing push-ups – either on the individual or the whole of the team! Remember that sprinting 10 to 15 yards is an important part of soccer.

2. Sprint relay with the ball

This is exactly the same as the previous exercise but this time, executed with the ball. See *illustration 307*. The ball is transferred over between the cones containing the file of players. Running with the ball as quickly as possible is again a valuable skill worth practising.

307

308

3. Multi-line relay with the ball

Cones are laid out in the manner shown in *illustration 308* approximately five yards between the lines. Teams of three are ideal but it will depend on the numbers of cones, players and balls you have available. With uneven numbers, have one player – the first – go twice, the second time as the last man.

The coach can employ a great many different relays with the multi-line set-up, and can enjoy a meaningful 20 minutes with his players practising ball manipulation on the run. The skill of manoeuvering the ball is an integral part of ball control and dribbling. With the multi-line situation, here are just some of the types of relays that can be used:

a. *Zigzag* – in and out, and finishing with a complete circle of the starting line cone before transferring to the next player. The circle of the cone prevents any cheating.

b. With the ball, the player makes a complete circle of the second cone, moves on and makes a complete circle of the third cone. He then moves on around the top cone, and sprints back with the ball around the starting line cone, making a complete circle before transferring the ball to the next person.

c. Left foot only or right foot only.

d. Any number of permutations and variations of a, b, and c.

The players have to concentrate carefully in order to understand the instructions as the relays can be changed by the coach each time.

4. Header relay

This relay involves two teams. The distance between the lines will depend on the age, physique and ability of the players but will be anything from five to 10 yards. The sequence is as follows: the first player

309

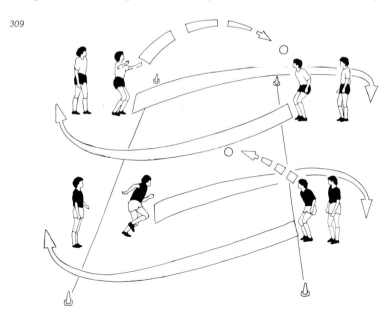

310

throws the ball head-high to the player opposite. He heads it back from behind his line to the third player who must receive it behind his line before throwing it to be headed by the fourth player. Each time a player throws or heads the ball, he follows it to the opposite side and to the back of the file, and continues the sequence from there (see *illustration 309*). This is an excellent practice for developing accuracy and power in heading.

5. *Keeping up (headers)*

Here, teams of five or six are ideal. There is no set distance between the groups. The objective is to keep the ball from hitting the ground by the use of the head (see *illustration 310*).

The rule is one-touch so that a player cannot have two consecutive headers. The sequence is strictly adhered to, and any player who tries to recover the situation of a poor header when he is out-of-turn will terminate the team's attempt. The winner is the team that gains the greatest number of consecutive headers:

1. The practice should be started by a throw – either to the opposite person, or by the player to himself.
2. Players having headed the ball can either join the back of the opposite file or go to the back of their own file (the coach can decide this – if there are only four in a team, it's better if they go to the back of their own file because of time limitations). This will help develop accuracy and technique in heading.

There are any number of relays to practise, and the coach should be able to concoct a few good ones of his own by taking into account the facilities that are available. They needn't be too strictly soccer-related as their natural emphasis on sprinting and teamwork already make relays beneficial to players.

Summary

The coach's first priority is *not* to entertain the players but to help them develop their soccer abilities both as individuals and as team members. Still, the coach who ignores the fun aspect of practice sessions is making a great mistake. The object is to keep the sessions bubbling from start to finish. Although there will be times when more serious practice or a chalk talk is desirable – perhaps necessary – remember to administer the medicine in small doses. All players want to learn by doing. And the younger the player, the less he can assimilate. For this reason, keep the talk to a minimum.

Conditioned games and practices have great value, so learn to use these tools wisely. And now it's back to practice. Offer a guiding hand and a ready smile, and most of all, enjoy your players.

Index